The Beatles
The Days Of Their Life

The Beatles

The Days Of Their Life

SUNDAY NOV. 10TH

THE BEATLES

ALL SEATS & STANDING
ROOM COMPLETELY

SOLD OUT

CHARTWELL
BOOKS, INC.

First published in 2010 by

CHARTWELL BOOKS, INC.
A Division of
BOOK SALES, INC.
276 Fifth Avenue Suite 206
New York, New York 10001

ISBN 13: 978-0-7858-2701-6
ISBN 10: 0-7858-2701-3

Copyright © 2011 Greene Media Ltd.
34 Dean Street, Brighton, East Sussex, BN1 3EG, UK

The information in this book is true and complete to the best
of our knowledge. All recommendations are made without
any guarantee on the part of the author or Publisher, who also
disclaim any liability incurred in connection with the use of this
data or specific details.

We recognize, further, that some words, model names, and
designations mentioned herein are the property of the
trademark holder. We use them for identification purposes only.
This is not an official publication.

Compiled and written by Richard Havers

Designed by Angela Ball and Dave Ball at daviball@sky.com

All Internet site information provided was correct when
provided by the Author. The Publisher can accept no
responsibility for this information becoming incorrect.

Printed and bound in China

Reprinted 2011, 2012, 2013

Contents

Foreword

The first time I played on stage with the Beach Boys was on April 9, 1965, right around the time the Beatles' *Eight Days A Week* was in the Billboard Top 10. A week or so later *Help Me Rhonda* started to make its way up the Hot 100, but it was soon overtaken by the Beatles' *Ticket to Ride* which made No.1 during the third week in May. On the last week of May *Help Me Rhonda* replaced the Beatles as the No.1 song in America.

Having been a part of the California music scene for what seemed like a long time to me, I had been asked to join the Beach Boys to replace Brian on the road, as he wanted to concentrate his time, and his amazing talents, on creating music for the band to record. I sang Brian's falsetto parts on stage but my first problem was finding a microphone I could reach. Al Jardine's was way too low, Dennis Wilson was way back on the drum riser, Mike Love was the lead singer so he didn't share and I was not quite tall enough for Carl Wilson's mic. We played Memphis and I went down to Lansky's on Beale Street, the place where Elvis bought his clothes, and bought myself a pair of dark blue suede 'Beatle boots' that made me a couple of inches taller. I was now able to share a mic with Carl (my height issue solved) and four decades on, thanks to those 'Beatle boots' I'm still touring as a member of The Beach Boys, but these days I have my own microphone and...shoes!

Over the course of the next year I became an integral part of the Beach Boys. I sang on three hit albums, *Summer Days (And Summer Nights)*, *The Beach Boys Party* and *Pet Sounds*. During the thirteenth month of being in the band I saw a little open time where I could take a trip to London. Derek Taylor, who had worked for the Beatles but was now our publicist in Los Angeles, set up several print and radio interviews for me to do in London to publicize the Beach Boys. I arrived at Heathrow on Monday, May 16, 1966, carrying a copy *Pet Sounds* that had been released back in the States that very day – well in advance of its UK release.

The following day Kim Fowley, my great friend from Los Angeles, who was by this time living in London and working in PR, began

delivering journalists to my suite at the Waldorf where I regaled them with tracks from *Pet Sounds*. I met Tony Rivers early on in the week and he introduced me to Keith Moon of the Who. Keith and I became fast friends and I now had Keith showing me rock 'n' roll night life in 1966 London. It was mad and wonderful and it ended with me going to see the Who in Windsor where I witnessed Keith start a fight with Pete and Roger...but that's a whole other story!

Saving the best for last: I arrived back at my hotel on my final evening in London and I found that John and Paul (courtesy of Keith Moon) were waiting for me in my suite. They were dressed very cool, in mod clothes, and after a short chat they sat down and I played the *Pet Sounds* album for them in its entirety, not once but twice! Later I learned that John and Paul went straight back to Paul's place and under the influence, so to speak, of Brian's incredible music they wrote *Here, There and Everywhere*.

Now don't get me wrong. I'm not saying the Beatles copied the Beach Boys but it was a time of great musical creativity and there were musical cross-currents happening everywhere. There's no way that John and Paul were copying *Pet Sounds*, they perhaps synthesized the gentle lyrical spirit of *Wouldn't it Be Nice* but there's no doubt that the Beach Boys music was in their musical ether when they came to work on *Sgt. Pepper's*.

When we recorded the *Beach Boys Party* album we sang *You've Got To Hide Your Love Away*, *I Should Have Known Better* and *Tell Me Why*. Little did I know that in December 1967, when I was in London with Mike Love, we would end up at the Beatles fancy dress party to celebrate the making of *Magical Mystery Tour*. I went dressed in a Sgt. Pepper's costume and towards the end of the evening Mike and I were on stage singing with the Beatles. If only someone had had a camera...even a phone with a camera would have been good!

When all is said and done I'm just a fellow musician who, like many others, loves the Beatles' music, loved them as people and have huge respect for their amazing legacy.

Bruce Johnston
THE BEACH BOYS

Best wishes
from
The Beatles

Ringo Starr

George Harrison

Paul McCartney

John Lennon

Something About The Beatles

Close to the end of the last century that quintessentially English band, Stackridge recorded a wonderful song called, *Something About The Beatles*.

"Turning on, tuning in, everyone believing in love. Making the world go round."

Just like everyone else on the planet, for the past half century, Stackridge felt that John, Paul, George and Ringo, collectively, The Beatles, made the world go round...and not just the world of music. There really was something about the Beatles that seemed to reach out to everyone. From royalty, to those who simply wanted to touch them, share the same air as them or if all else failed simply to buy the records and bathe in their melodies and their words.

So what do we know about The Beatles?

• Ringo was 70 in July 2010 and John would have been 70 in October of the same year... it hardly seems possible.

• *Love Me Do* came out on 5 October 1962; stories abound that Brian Epstein bought 10,000 copies for sale through his record shops – a story John Lennon always specifically denied.

• In April 1964 The Beatles held twelve positions on the American *Billboard* singles' chart.

• In 1964 The Beatles sold 25 million records in America alone; with global sales of around 80 million.

• *Can't Buy Me Love* sold 940,225 copies on the day of its release.

• 20 August 1969 was the last time that all four Beatles recorded together, they finished *I Want You (She's So Heavy)*.

• By 1969 world wide sales of Beatles records had topped 300 million.

• In the UK The Beatles have topped the album charts with fifteen different albums.

• In America there have been 20 singles that topped the *Billboard* Hot 100; there have been 19 albums that topped the *Billboard* album charts.

• In the UK the band have 4 Multi-Platinum albums, 4 Platinum albums, 8 Gold albums and 1 Silver album.

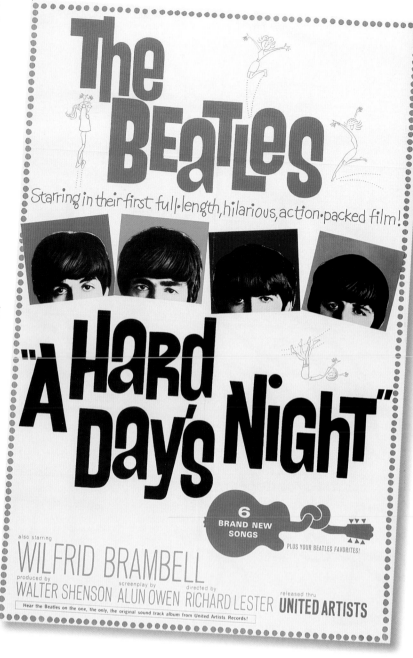

"We were just writing songs à la Everly Brothers, à la Buddy Holly, pop songs with no more thought of them than that—to create a sound. And the words were almost irrelevant."

JOHN LENNON

• The semaphore letters that the four Beatles are spelling out with their arms does not say H E L P, but N U J V.

• The Beatles had four less No.1 albums in Britain than America and two less British best selling singles.

• Other countries in which they have had the most No.1s include, Australia, Germany, Holland, Sweden, Canada and Norway.

• The Beatles had eight No.1 hits in Zimbabwe and Switzerland, but only two in Ethiopia.

• *A Hard Day's Night* is the first album entirely written by the Beatles – all thirteen tracks are by Lennon & McCartney.

• Paul McCartney filed a suit to dissolve The Beatles on 31 December 1970; the final dissolution of the partnership occurred in 1975.

• The Beatles have won seven Grammy Awards.

• They have sold more albums in America than any other artist.

• The Beatles first album, *Please Please Me*, took just ten hours to record.

• From starting to record *Sgt Pepper's Lonely Hearts Club Band* until it was completed took 129 days and 700 hours studio time.

• *Sgt Pepper's Lonely Hearts Club Band* established the trend for artists to include their lyrics within the LP's design.

• There are seventy famous people on the cover of *Sgt Pepper's Lonely Hearts Club Band* including, Oscar Wilde, Marilyn Monroe, Bob Dylan and Karlheinz Stockhausen.

• The Beatles have been named, collectively, as among the 20th Century's most influential people.

• The first Lennon & McCartney composition to top the UK singles chart by another artist was Billy J Kramer and the Dakotas' *Bad To Me* in August 1963.

• The first Lennon & McCartney composition to top the US singles chart by another artists was *A World Without Love* by Peter and Gordon in June 1964.

• *She Loves You* sold over 750,000 copies in under four weeks after its release.

• The Beatles first album, *Please Please Me* album topped the charts for 30 weeks before being replaced by *With The Beatles*, which stayed there for 21 weeks.

• Of the fourteen tracks on *Please Please Me* only eight were written by them. On *With the Beatles* seven songs were not written by them – one of the seven, *Don't Bother Me,* was by George Harrison

• George Harrison sings lead vocals on two of the tracks on the *Please Please Me* album.

• The Beatles received fifteen Ivor Novello Awards from the British Academy of Songwriters, Composers and Authors.

"When the Beatles split up, I felt on the rocks. I was accused of walking out on them, but I never did. I think we were all pretty weird at the time of the court cases."

PAUL MCCARTNEY

• George Martin played piano on almost every Beatles' album.

• *Beatles For Sale* can justifiably be nominated as the album that gave us folk-rock.

• The band's name was decided upon as a tribute to Buddy Holly.

• Six of the fourteen tracks on *Beatles For Sale* are cover versions – they are all American rock 'n' roll records that were seminal influences on the Beatles.

• *From Me To You* is the shortest Beatles single clocking in at one minute and 57 seconds.

• While the soundtrack to *Help!* was The Beatles fifth UK album it was their seventh Capitol album in America.

• The cover of *Revolver* was drawn by Klaus Voorman in the style of Aubrey Beardsley.

• *The Magical Mystery Tour* soundtrack was released as a double EP with a 28 page booklet in the UK. Somewhat against the band's wishes Capitol released it as an LP in America.

• The first Lennon & McCartney composition to chart in America was Del Shannon's cover of *From Me To You.*

• There are more than 3,000 recorded versions of Paul McCartney's *Yesterday*

• In the USA The Beatles have 6 Diamond albums, as well as 24 Multi-Platinum albums, 39 Platinum albums and 45 Gold albums.

• Eric Clapton plays lead guitar on *While My Guitar Gently Weeps.* George and Eric first met at Christmas 1964 during the Beatles Christmas Show on which the Yardbirds, in which Clapton played, also appeared.

• After the inclusion of Larry William's *Dizzy Miss Lizzy* on the *Help!* album every composition would be a Beatles' original on subsequent albums.

• The last song of their last concert on 29 August 1966 at San Francisco's Candlestick Park was *Long Tall Sally.*

• *Back in The USSR* from *The White Album* was a homage to both Chuck Berry and the Beach Boys (who paid homage themselves to old flat top on a number of occasions. According to Mike Love of the Beach Boys he encouraged McCartney to "talk about the girls all around Russia, the Ukraine and Georgia."

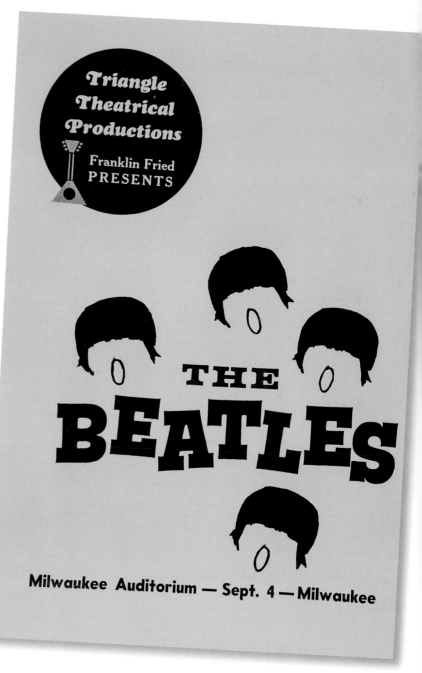

"Now that we were only playing in the studio and not anywhere else, we haven't got a clue what we're going to do. We have to start from scratch, thrashing it out in the studio, doing it the hard way."

GEORGE HARRISON TALKING ABOUT THE MAKING OF BEATLES FOR SALE

So there they are, some things – many things – about The Beatles. The greatest band the world has ever had. But perhaps above all, the one thing that we can be certain of is that there never was, nor ever, probably, will be, a band who were photographed more often than the Beatles. They came under the scrutiny of photographers everywhere they went. It has allowed us to bear witness to their evolution in a truly remarkable fashion. To watch them change, literally, before our very eyes. Those 'nice boys the Beatles' morphed into long-haired hippies that had mothers tutting from Liverpool to Lubbock and everywhere in between.

The Beatles physical evolution was the product of a whole mess of influences – not least because the Sixties was a time when anything seemed possible, even if it was often happening to other people, rather than you and me and the other mere mortals who watched it all unfolding through our TV screens and off the pages of music magazines and papers.

If there was, is, one thing about the Beatles, then it has to be how much happiness they have given to so many of us – then, now and forever. It's noticeable too how happy they seemed to be in so many of the photographs in this book. A cynic may say, who wouldn't be given what happened to them. But it is important to remember that they were a band that worked harder than just about any band...ever. It was not only the months on the road, but also the endless round of interviews, photo-calls, filming, and latterly the hours, days and months in the recording studio paving a way for every band, and artist, that has followed them.

And in the end?

Let it be . . .

Forever. . .

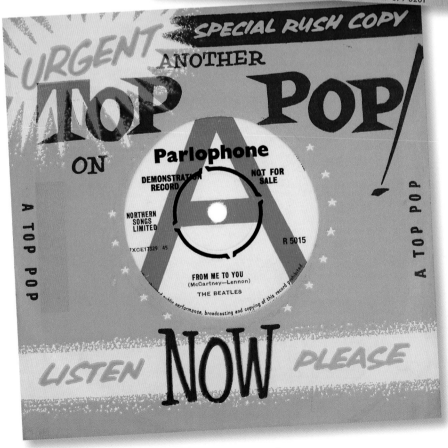

"If all four of us had to stand up in front of a million fans and they had to line up behind the one they liked best, I think Paul would get most, John and George would be joint second and Ringo would be last."

RINGO STARR

Over the Ocean

AS TEENAGERS the future Beatles do all the normal things that teenagers do and before long all four of them are playing music; initially it's Skiffle, that very British form of rock 'n' roll pioneered by Lonnie Donegan. When Paul meets John and joins the Quarrymen, followed shortly afterwards by his school friend George, the group start playing more rock 'n' roll and learning their craft before getting the chance to play in Hamburg's notorious red light district in August 1960. After returning from Germany the band are a polished unit able to compete with just about any group in Liverpool. Another visit in 1961 takes the Beatles up another rung on the ladder of success as they record with Tony Sheridan following which they return to Liverpool as conquering heroes...of sorts.

1934-61 TIMELINE

1934

September 19 Brian Samuel Epstein born in Liverpool.

1940

June 24 Stuart Sutcliffe born in Edinburgh.

July 7 Richard Starkey born in Liverpool.

October 9 John Winston Lennon born in Liverpool.

1942

June 18 James Paul McCartney born in Liverpool.

1943

February 25 George Harrison born in Liverpool.

1954

September September Paul met George on the bus on their way home from their school, The Liverpool Institute.

1956

Lonnie Donegan has hits with *Rock Island Line*, *Lost John* and *Bring A Little Water, Sylvie* – Skiffle is Britain's very own rock 'n' roll.

1957

Paul and George began playing guitars together in the Harrison's front room.

John starts a skiffle group, they eventually become the Quarrymen named after the school that most of its members attend.

July 6 Paul meets John at the Woolton Parish Church fete where the Quarrymen are playing Gene Vincent's *Be-Bop-A Lula*.

August 7 The Quarrymen play the Cavern for the first time.

October 18 Paul's first gig with the Quarrymen.

1958

January 24 Paul played the Cavern with the Quarrymen, a few weeks later George joined.

Autumn Cliff Richard has his first hit when *Move It* makes No.2 on the chart.

1959

September The Quarrymen begin playing regularly at the Casbah club in Liverpool; shortly after they change their name to Johnny & the Moondogs.

1960

January Stuart Sutcliffe joins Johnny & the Moondogs.

May They become The Silver Beatles (sometimes The Silver Beetles or The Silver Beats) and later in the month back Johnny Gentle on his tour of Scotland.

> **LATE NIGHT DANCE**
>
> BEAT BALLAD SHOW
> Presenting
> Star of TV and Decca Recording Fame—
> JOHNNY GENTLE and HIS GROUP.
> Supported by Scotland's Own Tommy Steele—
> ALEX. HARVEY and HIS BEAT BAND,
> With Ballad Singer—Bobby Rankine.
> To Entertain and Play For
> **DANCING**
> in the
> **TOWN HALL, ALLOA,**
> on
> **FRIDAY, 20th MAY,**
> 9.30 — 1.30.
> ADMISSION—Before 10 p.m., 4/-: after 10 p.m., 5/-.
>
> Buses After Dance to the HILLFOOTS DISTRICT.

August Pete Best becomes the new drummer.

August 17 The band arrive in Hamburg, having dropped 'silver' from their name, and play the Indra.

October Ringo is in Hamburg with Rory Storm and the Hurricanes and he, John, Paul and George play on a fun recording session with fellow Hurricane Walter Eymond.

November By this time The Beatles are playing The Kaiserkeller before George is deported from Germany for being under age; Paul and Pete follow a week later. John follows on but Stuart stays in Germany, which reduces the group to a foursome.

1961

January The Beatles begin playing frequent gigs around the Liverpool area .

April 1 The Beatles having arrived back in Hamburg a few days earlier begin a residency at the Top Ten Club; sometimes Stuart Sutcliffe, his hair brushed forward by then in what would become The Beatles' style, sits in with the band.

June 22 The Beatles back Tony Sheridan on *My Bonnie* and *The Saints* that become a single, as well as two other songs. The Beatles also record two songs by themselves: *Ain't She Sweet* and John and George's composition, *Cry For A Shadow.*

July 3 The Beatles arrive back in Liverpool and two weeks later start playing local gigs including the Cavern.

November 9 Brian Epstein visits the Cavern for the first time and sees the Beatles perform.

December 3 The Beatles have their first meeting with Brian about him becoming their manager; close to two weeks later they sign a deal.

Liverpool - Where it all started

In the 1950s, as John, Paul, George, Ringo, Pete and Stuart were growing up, Liverpool was a city of well over half a million people. It was a vibrant, multi-cultural city – home to Britain's first Chinatown. In the early 20th century the city was chronically short of housing, there was over crowding, and slums and although the council built more housing Liverpool suffered more than most in the 1930s.

During World War II Liverpool was a target for enemy bombing, almost 4,000 people died in Merseyside and more than 10,000 houses were destroyed. Many more people were seriously injured and a far greater number of homes were damaged.

After World War II the council cleared slums, rebuilt bombed out buildings and constructed overspill towns in the areas surrounding the city. Liverpool had a cultural identity, an attitude – it also had a seaport. Liners and cargo ships plied the North Atlantic and to all parts of what had been the British Empire. It is this melting pot that helped in the creation of the Beatles.

Located at the wide mouth of the Mersey River,
Liverpool was the ideal place for a port. In 1912
Liverpool had around 15% of the world's shipping
business and crucially, for the development of the
Beatles and the hundreds of other Liverpool bands
of the late 1950s and early 1960s, ships brought
music to Liverpool. Sailors and visitors brought
word of what was really happening in America,
even more crucially they brought with them
records – the likes of which you could not hear on
the staid old BBC.

Skiffle

In the 1950s Britain had its very own homemade musical genre, a music steeped in the blues, one that was an essential ingredient of the Sixties beat boom. For the Beatles and many other young men in late 1950's Britain, skiffle was a musical right of passage. Just like it has been for every generation, parental disapproval of teenage music was guaranteed to increase its popularity with teenagers – skiffle was way too raucous for anyone over the age of 30.

The Beatles started life as the Quarrymen, a skiffle group. This do-it-yourself musical craze may have had a short shelf life, but it was an inspiration – no one more so than the King of Skiffle – Lonnie Donegan. Skiffle made it possible for thousands of young Brits to dream of emulating their heroes, anyone could be a pop star. A guitar, a washboard and a tea-chest bass were all that was required.

BELOW: *The King of Skiffle, Lonnie Donegan*

ABOVE: *The Quarrymen – Eric Griffiths, Colin Hanton, Rod Davis, John Lennon, Pete Shotton and Len Garry – on 6 July 1957 at St. Peter's Woolton Parish Church in Liverpool*

The Cavern Club

The Beatles' spiritual home, the one place that everyone associates with the early days of the band. The Quarrymen first played the Cavern Club in January 1958, but the first time the Beatles were there in their own right was a lunchtime gig on 9 February 1961, they got £5 for their trouble. From then on the Beatles were back regularly; a little over a month later they played their first evening session. The pictures overleaf were taken in late 1961, after the band had been to Germany for their second visit.

RIGHT: *In 1961 the Beatles played around 250 gigs, a lot by the standards of any group. Among them was this one at the Tower Ballroom, one of the largest ballrooms on Merseyside; it could accommodate 5,000 people.*

OPERATiON
'Big Beat'
TOWER BALLROOM
NEW BRIGHTON
Friday, 10TH Nov. 1961
7.30 P.M. to 1.0 A.M.
★ Rocking to Merseysides TOP 5 GROUPS
The Beatles
Rory Storm and the Hurricanes
Gerry & The Pacemakers
The Remo Four
Kingsize Taylor and the Dominoes
2 LICENSED BARS (until 11.30 P.M.) BUFFET
Special Late Transport (L.POOL · WIRRAL · CHESHIRE)
TICKETS 5/- from RUSHWORTHS · LEWIS'S
CRANES · STOTHERS
TOWER BALLROOM

Like Dreamers Do

IT WAS IN **M**ARCH that the Beatles began wearing suits that Brian Epstein, their new manager had bought for them. The question of image was all-important to Epstein. The leather jackets would soon be consigned to the back of their respective wardrobes. After the disappointment of being turned down by Decca's Dick Rowe, who would later sign the Rolling Stones, the Beatles met the man who would justifiably be called 'the fifth Beatle'. George Martin was more at home with classical music, jazz and the comedians that were the most successful of Parlophone's recording artists. At Christmas the Beatles made the third trip of the year to Hamburg's Star Club, during which they honed their craft, it was to be their last extended visit. The Beatles would also get themselves a new drummer...

1962 TIMELINE

January 1   The Beatles audition for Decca.

January 3   Their first show of the year at the Cavern.

January 4   Voted Liverpool's top group in Mersey Beat Poll. Gerry & The Pacemakers voted second.

January 5   *My Bonnie* single is released on Polydor. It's billed as Tony Sheridan and the Beatles.

January 24   The Beatles sign their management contract with Brian Epstein at NEMS. Epstein gets 25% of their earnings, a good deal more than most managers.

February 8   The Beatles Decca audition tapes are made into acetates at HMV's shop in London's Oxford Street. It leads to the Beatles meeting EMI's publishing company head, Sid Coleman who encourages Epstein to meet with George Martin.

February 12   The Beatles audition for a BBC radio producer.

March 7   The Beatles record their first BBC radio show, it's for *Teenagers' Turn — Here we Go*; the show is broadcast the following day.

March 31   The Beatles play Stroud's Subscription Rooms, a rare foray outside the Liverpool area.

April 10   Stuart Sutcliffe dies in Hamburg.

April 13   The Beatles begin a seven week booking at Hamburg's Star Club.

April 23   *My Bonnie* gets a US release as Tony Sheridan and the Beat Brothers.

May 9   Brian Epstein meets George Martin in London.

June 6   The Beatles record *Besame Mucho*, *P.S. I Love You*, *Love Me Do* and *Ask Me Why* at Abbey Road for EMI. George Martin likes what he hears, except Pete Best's drumming and signs the band.

June 9   Beatles play the Cavern, their first Liverpool appearance in two months.

June 11   Another session for BBC radio's *Teenagers' Turn — Here We Go*; it's broadcast June 15.

June 21   The Beatles are on the bill with Bruce Channel at the Tower Ballroom, New Brighton.

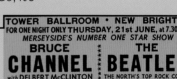

August 15   Pete Best plays his last gig with the Beatles at the Cavern.

August 18   Ringo Starr's first gig with the Beatles is at the Horticultural Society Dance in Port Sunlight, Birkenhead.

August 22   Granada Television film the Beatles at the Cavern but it is not shown at the time and is not broadcast until November 1963.

August 23   John Lennon marries Cynthia Powell after she reveals she is pregnant. In the evening the Beatles play Riverpark Ballroom, Chester.

September 4   The Beatles flew to London to record at Abbey Road for their first recording session since signing to EMI. They record *Love Me Do* and *How Do You Do It*.

September 5   Back in Liverpool for a Cavern gig.

September 11   Back at Abbey Road to record *Love Me Do, P.S. I Love You* and *Please Please Me* using session drummer, Andy White

October 1   The Beatles sign a five-year contract with Brian Epstein, he still gets 25% of their earnings.

October 5   UK single release – *Love Me Do/P.S. I Love You* on Parlophone 45R 4949.

October 8   The Beatles record an interview for Radio Luxembourg at EMI's Manchester Square HQ in London; it's broadcast October 12.

October 13   *Love Me Do* enters the UK singles chart.

October 17   The Beatles have their first TV appearance on Granada Television's *People and Places*.

October 25   The Beatles record *Love Me Do, A Taste of Honey* and *P.S I Love You* for the BBC's *Teenagers' Turn – Here we Go*; it's broadcast October 26.

October 29   A second appearance on Grenada Television's *People and Places* is recorded; it airs November 2.

November 1   The Beatles open at the Star Club in Hamburg for the first of 14 nights sharing the bill with Little Richard.

November 16   Home the previous day from Hamburg they are back recording an appearance on Radio Luxembourg's 'The Friday Spectacular'; it airs on November 23.

November 26   Beatles at Abbey Road to record *Please Please Me, Ask Me Why* and *Tip of My Tongue* (the tape of this was destroyed).

December 18   The Beatles start their last Hamburg residency; it lasts until New Year's Eve.

December 27   *Love Me Do* gets to No.17 on the UK singles chart, its highest position.

So Who Do We Need to Beat?

Back in May 1960 the Silver Beatles, as they were then calling themselves, had auditioned to become Billy Fury's backing band. Fury (below) was one of Britain's best rock 'n' rollers who in 1960 had five hit singles before his cover of *Halfway to Paradise* made No.3 in May 1961. Over the next two years Billy Fury had 7 Top 10 hits including the brilliant *Jealousy* that got to No.2 and the equally great, *Like I've Never Been Gone* which reached No.3. In 1960 he recorded his debut album, *The Sound of Fury*, which is one of the most exciting albums to come out of Britain in those pre-Beatle days. He was just one of the artists that the Beatles needed to beat if they were going to find success. Of course if they had become his backing group the world would be a very different place.

THE SOUND OF FURY • BILLY FURY MONO 8449902 DECC

the sound of FURY

ABOVE: In the first four months of 1963 Cliff Richard & The Shadows, either together or separately had 5 UK chart toppers.

ABOVE: After his discharge from the US Army in March 1960 Elvis had 9 UK No.1 singles before 1962 was over.

LEFT: Much admired by the Beatles, Don and Phil, the Everly Brothers had 6 UK top ten records, including three No.1s in the first couple of years of the Sixties.

LEFT: Two American's that influenced the Beatles were Gene Vincent (left) and Eddie Cochran. On Easter Sunday 1960 Cochran was killed in a car crash midway through a British tour with Gene Vincent. On the day that John met Paul he was playing Vincent's Be Bop A Lula; it was also the song that John played the only time his mother Julia saw him perform.

From the STAR CLUB, HAMBURG

THE BEATLES
SEND BEST WISHES TO
THEIR FANS AND FRIENDS

"We'll be back JANUARY 1, and our new single
is out on the 11th ———— see you!"

JOHN, PAUL, GEORGE and **RINGO**

Out and about

After the Decca audition and Brian Epstein signing the Beatles to a management deal he realized that they needed to break out of their Merseyside comfort zone if they were to become a real success. He knew he had to get them gigs in the rest of the country and his first foray 'down South' was a headline show at the Stroud Subscription Rooms, not everyone's idea of the capital of rock 'n' roll but it was a start. Two weeks later it was back to Hamburg for another residency at the Star Club (when the picture was taken that included Roy Young, who had his own band, on piano); meanwhile Ringo Starr was still with Rory Storm and the Hurricanes.

SUBSCRIPTION ROOMS
STROUD

SAT. 31ST MAR.
8.30 TO 11.45 P.M.

JAYBEE CLUBS present Liverpool's Top Vocal and Instrumental Group—Stars of Polydor Records—THE

SENSATIONAL
BEATLES

PLUS

THE REBEL ROUSERS

ADMISSION 5/- • REFRESHMENTS

BY COUNCIL REGULATION   NO TEDDY BOY SUITS

LADIES PLEASE BRING A CHANGE OF SHOES AS STILETTO HEELS ARE NOT ALLOWED

NO ADMISSION AFTER 10 P.M.

Next Week - LEE ATKINS!

By George, I Think They've Got It

On 6 June The Beatles went to Abbey Road to record for EMI. George Martin liked what he heard, except Pete Best's drumming; nevertheless he signs the band. Back in Liverpool it was business as usual with gigs all over Merseyside including the Tower Ballroom in New Brighton. The 15 August saw Pete Best play his last Beatles gig and three days later Ringo was in the vacant drum stool. On 23 August John married Cynthia Powell and in the evening the Beatles play Riverpark Ballroom, Chester. A little over a week later The Beatles flew to London to Abbey Road Studios for their first recording session since signing to EMI's Parlophone label. They recorded *Love Me Do* and *How Do You Do It*. A few days after that they were back at Abbey Road to record *Love Me Do*, *P.S. I Love You* and *Please Please Me* this time instead of using Ringo they used a session drummer named Andy White – Ringo played percussion. Three weeks later they sign a five-year deal with EMI and four days after that out comes The Beatles first single, *Love Me Do* backed by *P.S. I Love You*.

THE BEATLES

PARLOPHONE RECORDS

1963

Beatlemania - They Love Us

THE YEAR BEGAN inauspiciously with a mini-tour of Scotland at venues that included the Two Red Shoes Ballroom in Elgin; it ended with the Beatles hosting their own London Christmas show. In between the Beatles had sold millions of records, released two chart-topping albums, made countless radio and TV appearances, starred in a Royal Command performance, topped the bill at the London Palladium and Beatlemania was on course for becoming a worldwide phenomena.

1963 TIMELINE

January 1 After their last Hamburg Star Club booking the Beatles flew back to London.

January 2 The Beatles flew to Scotland for a short tour, but their plane was diverted from Edinburgh to Aberdeen – it caused the cancellation of their first gig in Keith. The tour ended on January 8 with a live appearance on Scottish TV.

January 11 UK Single release *Please Pease Me/Ask Me Why* on Parlophone 45-R 4983.

January 13 The Beatles recorded an appearance on ABC TV's 'Thank Your Lucky Stars' – their most important TV show to date – it aired on January 19.

January 19 *Please Please Me* enters the UK singles chart.

January 22 The Beatles recorded their first appearance on the BBC's 'Saturday Club'.

February 2 The first show of a package tour headlined by Helen Shapiro at Bradford's Gaumont Cinema.

February 11 A mammoth ten hour session at Abbey Road to record the tracks needed for the Beatles first album.

February 23 *Please Please Me* makes No.1 on some of the music paper charts but only No.2 on the Record Retailer chart.

February 25 US Single release *Please Please Me/Ask Me Why* on Vee Jay VJ498.

March 3 Last date of the Helen Shapiro tour at Gaumont Cinema in Hanley Staffordshire.

March 5 The Beatles record *From Me To You* at Abbey Road.

March 9 A second package tour, this time Tommy Roe and Chris Montez topping the bill, opens at the Grenada Cinema, East Ham, London. The Beatles soon take over the top spot.

March 16 A live appearance on the BBC's 'Saturday Club' before driving to Sheffield for their appearance on the package tour.

March 22 UK album release – *Please Please Me* on Parlophone PMC 1202 (mono) PCS 3042 (stereo).

March 31 The last night of the Montez-Roe package tour.

April 5 The Beatles are awarded a silver disc, their first, for the single, *Please, Please Me*. They play a short private set for EMI staffers.

April 8 John Charles Julian Lennon is born to John and Cynthia.

April 11 UK single release *From Me To You/Thank You Girl* on Parlophone R5105.

April 13 The Beatles meet Cliff Richard at the home of The Shadow's Bruce Welch.

April 14 The Beatles see the Rolling Stones play the Crawdaddy Club in Richmond.

April 18 The Beatles play the Royal Albert Hall in the Swinging Sounds '63 show with among others Del Shannon who heard them play *From Me To You* and recorded it soon after; it then became the first Lennon & McCartney song to make the US charts.

April 20 *From Me To You* enters the UK singles chart.

April 21 The NME's Poll Winners' All-Star Concert at Wembley – the Beatles appear despite not having won anything.

April 28 The Beatles have their first proper holiday in years. Paul, George and Ringo go to Tenerife for 12 days, while John accompanies Brian Epstein to Spain.

May 4 *From Me To You* makes No.1 on the UK singles chart.

May 18 A package tour with Roy Orbison begins at the Adelphi Cinema, Slough.

May 27 US Single release *From Me To You/Thank You Girl* on Vee Jay VJ522.

June 8 *My Bonnie* enters the UK singles chart, having been released by Polydor to capitalize on the band's success.

June 18 Paul's 21st birthday party at his aunt's home. John Lennon attacked Bob Wooler, a long time friend of the Beatles.

June 26 John & Paul wrote *She Loves You* in a hotel room in Newcastle – it would become the Beatles' first million seller.

July 1 The Beatles record *She Loves You* at Abbey Road.

July 12 UK EP release *Twist & Shout* on Parlophone GEP 8882 (*Twist And Shout, A Taste Of Honey, Do You Want To Know A Secret & There's A Place*.

July 18	The Beatles begin recording their second album at Abbey Road.
July 26	US album release *Introducing The Beatles* on Vee Jay VJLP1062.
August 1	The first issue of *The Beatles* monthly book goes on sale.
August 3	The Beatles last show at the Cavern.
August 12	A week long residency at the Odeon Cinema, Llandudno – two shows a night.
August 19	A week-long residency at the Gaumont Cinema Bournemouth.
August 23	UK single release *She Loves You/I'll Get You* on Parlophone R 5055.
August 26	A week-long residency at the Odeon Cinema, Southport.
August 31	*She Loves You* enters the UK singles chart.
September 14	*She Loves You* makes No.1 on the UK singles chart.
September 15	The Beatles appear at the Great Pop Prom at the Royal Albert Hall, London; the Rolling Stones are also on the bill.
September 16	The Beatles all go on holiday. John & Cynthia to Paris, George to visit his sister in Illinois USA. Paul, Jane Asher, his new girlfriend, Ringo and Maureen go to Greece.
October 4	The Beatles first appearance on 'Ready Steady Go!'
October 13	The Beatles appear on the prestigious *Sunday Night at the London Palladium* to an audience of over 15 million.
October 17	The Beatles record *I Want To Hold Your Hand* at Abbey Road.
October 23	The Beatles fly to Stockholm, Sweden, their first overseas gigs since becoming famous.

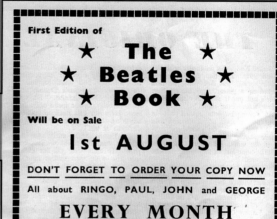

October 31   The Beatles arrive home at London's Heathrow Airport from Sweden to chaotic scenes. Ed Sullivan is leaving London at the same time and is amazed; so much so that he books them for his US TV show.

November 1   UK EP Release, The Beatles (No.1) Parlophone GEP 8883. The Odeon Cinema, Cheltenham, the first night of The Beatles' own headlining autumn tour.

November 4   The Beatles appear at the Royal Command Performance at London's Prince of Wales Theatre.

"GAD, SMITHERS, WHAT NEXT?"

November 16   Before the band's show at Bournemouth's Winter Gardens CBS interviewed the band and later CBS, ABC and NBC all filmed part of the concert.

November 22   UK album release – *With The Beatles* on Parlophone PMC 1206 (mono) PCS 3045 (stereo).

November 29   November 29 UK single release *I Want To Hold Your Hand/This Boy* on Parlophone R 5084. There were advance sales of over one million before release.

December 7   *I Want To Hold Your Hand* enters the UK singles chart.

December 13   The last date of the autumn tour at the Gaumont Cinema, Southampton.

December 14   *I Want To Hold Your Hand* tops the UK chart for the first of five weeks at No.1.

December 21   The first Beatles Christmas show preview at the Gaumont Cinema, Bradford.

December 24   The Beatles Christmas Show opens at the Astoria Cinema, Finsbury Park, London.

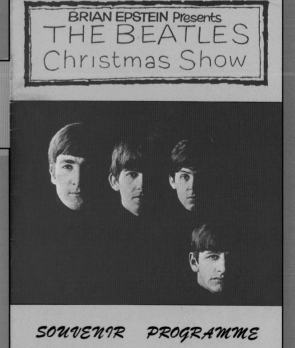

BRIAN EPSTEIN Presents THE BEATLES Christmas Show

SOUVENIR PROGRAMME

December 26   US Single release *I Want To Hold Your Hand/I Saw Her Standing There* on Capitol 5112.

ON THE RECORD

POPLAND GOES BRITISH . .

by PATRICK DONCASTER

IT might look black and white to you. But today's Pop Thirty drips with red, white and blue.

EIGHT of the top TEN discs are British.

FIFTEEN of the top TWENTY are home made. Only in the last ten of the thirty do the Americans get any sway.

Even Elvis, with his first-rate "Return to Sender," returns three paces down the hit ladder in face of the British onslaught. Week by week the British Discland scene bristles with new names. Some of them stay.

This time last year few of you had ever heard of the Tornados (they were formed only in December, 1961), Mike Sarne (his first disc reached No. 1 last July) or Susan Maughan.

Now they are established names in Discland.

There are more on the way, queuing up for fame.

WATCH the Beatles, a guitar-based instrumental quartet from Liverpool with a style of their own.

Their first British disc (they made one in Germany) hit the scene last October—"Love Me Do." It was a success and only this week makes its exit from the chart.

PLEASING!

Now here they come with their follow-up: "Please Please Me" (Parlophone).

It should please you.

On the same label in come the Federals—another instrumental and vocal group. They are six lads who started out as a rock group in the Watford area, calling themselves the Beatniks—"the accent was on the beat, not the cult," they explain.

They changed their name, they changed their style. Now they take "Brazil" and make an exciting Latin-American feast of it.

A TREBLE?

There is also a new boy named Ben Richmond bowing in on Piccadilly.

Ben, 21, from London's Limehouse, makes dartboards by day.—"I stick the numbers on," he says. By night he sings in clubs and at dance-halls.

He could well cut up a score with "Blue Bird."

The Beatles . . . a guitar - based quartet with expressions suitable for having just dropped out of the charts. But they've got a follow-up on the way.   LEFT to RIGHT: George Harrison, John Lennon, Paul McCartney, Ringo Starr.

ABOVE: *After a short tour of Scotland in early January it was back to playing gigs in such diverse venues as the Civic Hall in the Wirral for the Wolverham Welfare Association, the El Rio Club in Macclesfield and of course the Cavern. Pictured at Majestic Ballroom, Birkenhead The Beatles, under Epstein's management, were expected to be smart, although Ringo seems to believe that keeping his tie done up is not part of 'the uniform'.*

LEFT: *On 24 January the band had one of their first ever mentions in the national press.*

ABOVE: *Helen Shapiro had her first hit when she was 14 years old in 1961 with the aptly named Don't Treat Me Like a Child. Before the year was out she had topped the charts twice with You Don't Know and the one that everyone remembers – Walkin' Back To Happiness. Voted Britain's most popular female singer she had four chart hits in 1962. As the tour opened Please Please Me entered the charts, half way through the tour it was No.1 and The Beatles were closing the first half.*

RIGHT: *On 2 February when the Helen Shapiro tour opened the Beatles were definitely not, as some have claimed, bottom of the bill, that honour has to go to The Red Price Band followed by The Honeys*

ABOVE: *On April 5 the Beatles played a short lunchtime set for Parlophone and EMI executives at EMI House in London's Manchester Square at which they were presented with their first silver disc for Please Please Me. Later that evening they played The Swimming Baths at Leyton. Since recording their appearance on Thank Your Lucky Stars they had played 41 different gigs, often two shows a night, appeared on radio, been in the recording studio, done interviews and photo sessions – all in the space of 46 days.*

LEFT: *On 17 February the band were at Teddington Studios to record their second appearance on Thank Your Lucky Stars. Pictured with them are the Vernon's Girls who also came from Liverpool. The show aired on 23 February with The Beatles singing Please Please Me.*

ABOVE: *Wearing their new 'Beatles jackets' the band were presented with their silver disc by George Martin,*

"One of these days we must sort through our old compositions. We might be sitting on a goldmine."

JOHN

LEFT: *Two days after John and Cynthia's son Julian was born the band were back relatively close to home to play the Majestic Ballroom, Birkenhead, just across the Mersey from Liverpool. With The Beatles increasing popularity their ability to play what were relatively small shows was becoming increasingly limited. Brian Epstein booked this show well in advance of their booming popularity and so he was just honouring a contract. Ringo's drum kit still displays the old Beatles' logo.*

BELOW: *After a holiday in late April and early May when John went on holiday to Spain with Brian Epstein and Ringo, Paul and George went to Tenerife the band went straight back on the road. After a few ballroom gigs their next package tour opened, this one starring Roy Orbison; after a few nights the Beatles were topping the bill.*

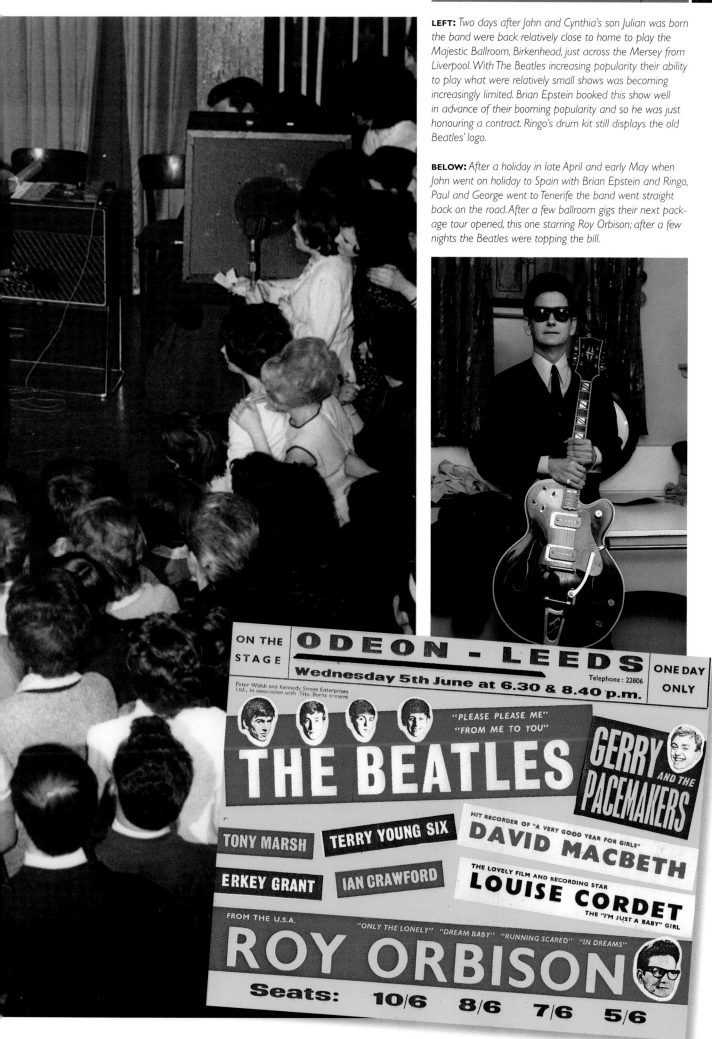

ON THE STAGE **ODEON - LEEDS** ONE DAY ONLY
Wednesday 5th June at 6.30 & 8.40 p.m. Telephone : 22806

Peter Walsh and Kennedy Street Enterprises Ltd., in association with Tito Burns present

"PLEASE PLEASE ME" "FROM ME TO YOU"

THE BEATLES

GERRY AND THE PACEMAKERS

TONY MARSH   TERRY YOUNG SIX

HIT RECORDER OF "A VERY GOOD YEAR FOR GIRLS" **DAVID MACBETH**

ERKEY GRANT   IAN CRAWFORD

THE LOVELY FILM AND RECORDING STAR **LOUISE CORDET** THE "I'M JUST A BABY" GIRL

FROM THE U.S.A. "ONLY THE LONELY" "DREAM BABY" "RUNNING SCARED" "IN DREAMS"

ROY ORBISON

Seats: 10/6   8/6   7/6   5/6

"Hands nonchalantly in pockets of slim-line trousers, rhythm-tapping feet encased in elastic sided boots, thirteen of the most listened-to young men in Britain get together for the first time."

DAILY MIRROR 21 JUNE 1963

Liverpool Impresario's Beat Bands

In June the *Daily Mirror*'s photographer was invited to Liverpool to photograph Brian Epstein with his three leading beat groups for a story entitled – The Liverpool Sound. John, Paul, Ringo and George, Gerry and the Pacemakers: Gerry Marsden, Freddie Marsden, Les Chadwick and Les McGuire, and Billy J Kramer and the Dakotas: Robin McDonald, Mike Maxfield, Billy J Kramer, Ray Jones and Tony Mansfield. It was June 18, Paul's 21st birthday and everyone went back to Paul's Aunt Jinny's for a party held in a marquee in the garden.

BELOW: *The week starting Monday 22 July the band were in Weston-super-Mare to play the Odeon Cinema in the evening but took time out to have they photograph taken on the beach dressed in antique style bathing costumes – there is no sign of them being bored with the attention of the camera at this point. A little over a week later they were playing one of their, by now, less frequent ballroom gigs. 2,000 fans packed into the Imperial for their second show at the venue that was to burn down in 1976.*

IMPERIAL BALLROOM - NELSON

THE BALLROOM OF THE STARS - NOW WITH LICENSED BAR

presents

WEDNESDAY, JULY 31ST 1963
7·30 P.M. TILL 11·30 P.M. (DOORS OPEN 6·30)

THE WORLD'S NO. 1 GROUP

THE BEATLES

PLUS: FULL SUPPORTING GROUPS

TICKETS: FROM AGENTS 7/6 AT THE DOOR 8/6

TICKETS at — Burnley – Electron Radio Co. 2. Hall Street. Off the Centre; Brierfield – Fell, Newsagent, The Centre; Nelson – Multi Relays; Reed's, Butchers Market Square; The Coffee Pot, Manchester Road; Barnoldswick – Holt's Shoe Shop; Colne – Rabino's Snack Bar, Skipton Road Top. Padiham – Duffy's Record Centre; Barrowford – J S Holmes, Newsagent, 108, Gisburn Road; Earby – Mason's Greengrocers; Imperial Ballroom, Nelson 65760.

LATE TRANSPORT ON MAIN ROAD THROUGH BURNLEY TO MEMORIAL GARDENS PADIHAM and MAIN ROADS THROUGH COLNE TO BARNOLDSWICK

SATURDAY, AUGUST 3RD SENSATIONAL SHOWNIGHT
7·30 – 11·30 Licensed Bar
Late Transport to all parts

RIGHT: *All good things come to an end and when the Beatles played the last of their 300 shows at the Cavern on Saturday 3 August the place was packed – tickets had sold out with 30 minutes. The picture was taken in February 1963*

The Beatles Meet Fleet Street

Brian Epstein wanted his group to be more than just popular with kids, he wanted them to be 'light entertainers'. Donald Zec was the doyen of Fleet Street show business writers who had met everyone from Marilyn Monroe to Frank Sinatra, Danny Kaye to Clark Gable and liked to count many of them as his friends. It was a coup for the Beatles to go round to his apartment and be interviewed on his sofa in September 1963 as *She Loves You* was topping the British charts.

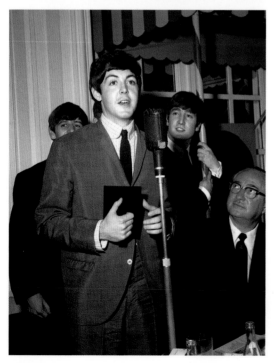

ABOVE AND LEFT: *In early September the Beatles attended a luncheon at the Savoy Hotel in London hosted by the Variety Club of Great Britain. They were there to receive what was their first national award, one that acknowledged that they were becomming a force in the music business. With them that day were Billy J Kramer and Susan Maughan; Susan had a big hit with her cover of Bobby's Girl in 1962 – despite appearances she was younger than all of the Beatles except George.*

RIGHT: *Five days after lunch at the Savoy the band were at the Royal Albert Hall in London for the Great Pop Prom show. Also on the bill were The Rolling Stones, sporting their natty leather waistcoats that their manager, Andrew Loog Oldham, had insisted they buy in order to have a similar image to the Beatles... and just about every other band.*

Fans or Fanatics?

A picture of innocence? Taken backstage, with Rona Campbell from Fiji and Jennifer Gemmell at the Carlton Theatre in Kirkcaldy, Scotland on 6 October where 3,000 fans watched their two performances.

ALBERT A. BONICI
presents

THE
BEATLES
Scottish Tour
1963

GLASGOW
KIRKCALDY
DUNDEE

SOUVENIR

2/-

RIGHT: *The Beatles topped the bill at Sunday Night at The London Palladium on 13 October and outside the fans gathered in massive numbers, despite not having tickets to get in. This show was the beginning of the craziness that followed the Beatles around for the next few years. 15 million viewers tuned in to see them play, in black and white of course, From Me To You, I'll Get You, She Loves You and Twist And Shout.*

Fanatics!

On October 19 at a show at The Pavilion Gardens in Buxton things really did get out of hand and the police stopped the band from playing to prevent things turning ugly. It turned out to be the band's last ballroom gig, after that it was just cinemas – venues at which the stage was easier to defend! A month earlier they had played the Public Hall in Preston (main picture) where, despite it being a similar kind of venue, things had stayed relatively under control.

THE Beatles!

EUROPAS I SÄRKLASS POPULÄRASTE POPBAND! MED SIN "TWIST AND SHOUT" HAR DE GJORT EN SAGOLIK KOMETKARRIÄR. DE KOMMER NU FÖR FÖRSTA GÅNGEN TILL SVERIGE OCH VISAR UPP SIN FANTASTISKA SCEN-SHOW, SOM ÖVERALLT FÖRSÄTTER PUBLIKEN I FULL EXTAS!

EUROPAS POPBAND NUMMER ETT

KUNGL. TENNISHALLEN 26 OKT. kl. 17 & 20

ABOVE AND LEFT: *Back from a mini-tour of Sweden the scenes at London Airport on 31 October were unprecedented, it was what everyone was going to have to get used to over the next few years. Ed Sullivan was on his way through the airport at the same time and it convinced him that he needed this band on his US TV show.*

By Royal Command

ABOVE AND RIGHT: *In rehearsals during the afternoon at the Prince of Wales Theatre.*

It was, in publicity terms, arguably the biggest night of their career to date. The annual *Royal Variety Show* in front of members of the royal family, was watched in almost every home in Britain that had a TV set – those who did not have one went to a neighbour to watch it. While the Beatles appeared seventh on the bill – there were 18 other acts including Harry Secombe, topping the bill with his Pickwick show, Marlene Dietrich and Tommy Steele – it was the Beatles who stole the show. John's famous introduction to their last song was *the* moment of the Beatles' early TV career – the one that everyone watching talked about the following day. "For our last number I'd like to ask your help. The people in the cheaper seats clap your hands. And the rest of you, if you'd just rattle your jewellery. We'd like to sing a song called, *Twist And Shout*."

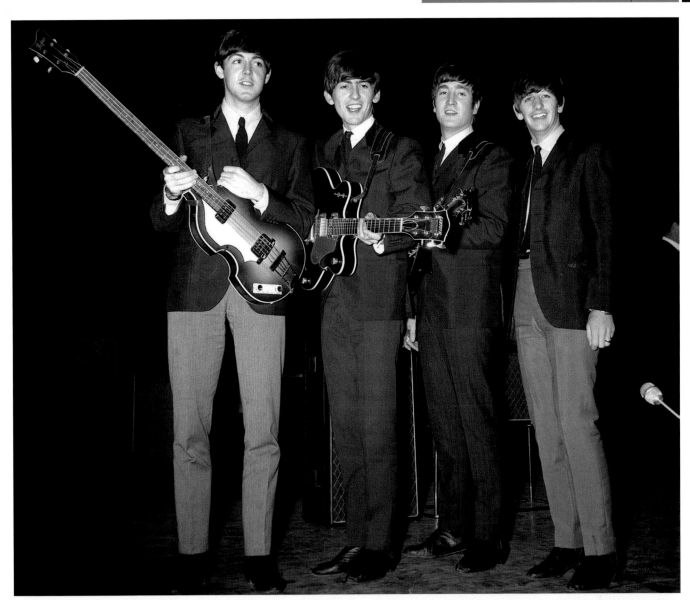

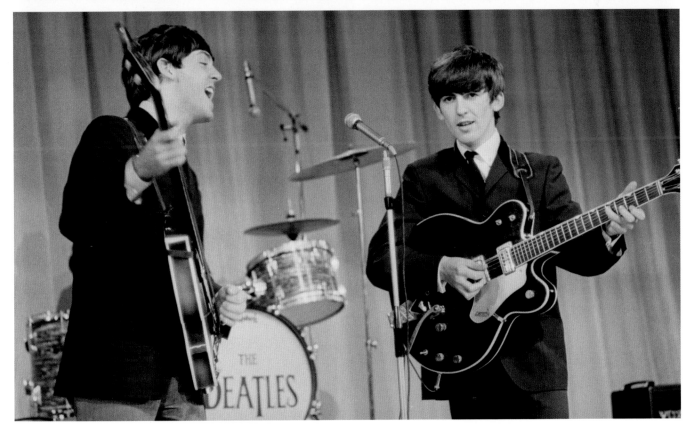

BELOW: *Being introduced to Princess Margaret, who attended the show along with the Queen Mother. At 33 Princess Margaret was probably the only senior member of the royal family who got close to understanding the Beatles.*

RIGHT: *The after-show party.*

Royal Performance in the presence of Her Majesty The Queen Mother on the Evening of Monday November 4th 1963 at The Prince of Wales Theatre, London.

PAGES 68 & 69: *The show itself, with the Beatles and the rest of the cast singing God Save The Queen.*

When Beatlemania Really Began

It was on The Beatles' first headlining tour of the UK that Beatlemania officially began. The term was coined by a *Daily Mirror* journalist, who was attempting to put into words the scenes he witnessed on the first night of their five-week tour at the Odeon Cinema in sleepy, conservative Cheltenham. From then on it just got crazier!

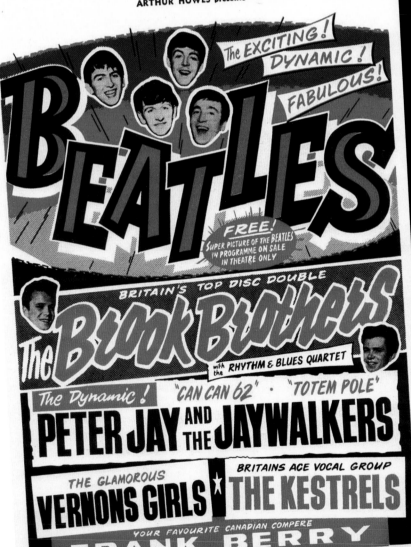

Making an Entrance (or an Exit)

Getting in and out of the venues became increasingly challenging as the tour went on. The local police in each town and city had their work cut out keeping the Beatles safe and the fans from getting hurt.

Two Shows Nightly

Their set was:

I Saw Her Standing There
From Me To You
All My Loving
You Really Got A Hold On Me
Roll Over Beethoven
Boys
Till There Was You
She Loves You
Money (That's What I Want)
Twist And Shout.

The fans

"We'll try to do everything we can to please you with the type of songs we write next year."
PAUL

Thank You, and Goodnight

They closed each night with *Twist and Shout* and always bowed low after finishing each number. As the curtains closed they played a short instrumental version of *From Me To You*

Liverpool Lads

As their autumn tour was nearing its end they appeared on TV on Grenada's *Scene* being interviewed with fellow Liverpudlian Ken Dodd, a comedian and singer. A few days later they filmed an appearance on *The Morcambe and Wise Show*; The Beatles closed the show wearing striped blazers and singing *Moonlight Bay* with their hosts. Five days later they were at Liverpool's Empire Theatre to by filmed as the four panellists on the BBC's *Juke Box Jury* with the show's host, David Jacobs. The audience of 2,500 was composed entirely of Beatles Fan Club members. George spent the night before at home with his parents where his Dad gave him breakfast; Ringo stayed at his parents' home on Admiral Grove and was spotted in the street making his way to the theatre. On Tuesday 17 December The Beatles recorded another appearance on *Saturday Club*, the BBC's long running pop show at the Playhouse Theatre in London, with Paul was Jane Asher, probably the first of the many times they were photographed together.

The All-Merseybeat; *Thank Your Lucky Stars*

On December 21 the Beatles topped the bill on the all Merseybeat edition of *Thank Your Lucky Stars*. They recorded it at Alpha studios in Birmingham on Sunday 15 December. The Beatles mimed to *She loves You*, *All My Loving*, *Twist and Shout* and *I Want to Hold Your Hand*. They are shown opposite on their 20 October appearance on the show.

LONDON ITV

1.15—News. **1.20** SPORTSTIME: Tenpin Bowling from Jarrow; Swimming from Llanelly; Racing Results; Professional Wrestling from Wallasey; Full Soccer Results.

5.15—Emerald Soup (serial): Final episode. **5.45** News.

5.50—THANK YOUR LUCKY STARS: With The Beatles, Billy J. Kramer and the Dakotas, Gerry and the Pacemakers, The Searchers, Cilla Black, Tommy Quickly, The Breakaways, and Brian Matthew.

6.35—BONANZA: The Legacy, with Lorne Greene.

7.30—THE SENTIMENTAL AGENT (adventure series): A Box of Tricks, with Carlos Thompson.

ABOVE: *Some of the other Liverpool stars that appeared on the show, Billy J Kramer and the Dakotas (left), The Searchers (right) and Cilla Black.*

RIGHT: *The Beatles with a young fan.*

> "We're looking forward to a holiday The pace of being a Beatle? It's like any other job."

JOHN LENNON

Merry Christmas!

On 21 December the first of the Beatles Christmas Shows had its first preview at the Gaumont Cinema in Bradford, the following night the second preview was at the Empire Theatre in Liverpool. On Christmas Eve it transferred to the Astoria Cinema in Finsbury Park, London where it ran until 11 January. Besides the Beatles the variety show included the Barron Knights with Duke D'Mond, The Fourmost, Tommy Quickly, Cilla Black, Billy J Kramer & The Dakotas and Rolf Harris. With two shows a night almost 100,000 people got to see it.

1964

A Hard Eight Days A Week

THIS WAS THE YEAR when the Beatles seemed to be working eight days a week – they really were here, there and everywhere. Apart from touring in the UK the band visited America for the first time and appeared on the *Ed Sullivan Show*. In the summer they toured America and at other times in the year played in Paris, Sweden, Denmark, Holland, Hong Kong, Australia and New Zealand. If all that was not enough there were numerous TV shows and many days and nights in the recording studio.

1964 TIMELINE

January 1 The Beatles performing *She Loves You* is shown on US TV on *The Jack Paar Show* – the first time the Beatles are seen by America.

January 11 The final night of the Beatles Christmas Show at London's Finsbury Park Astoria.

January 12 The Beatles appear on *Sunday Night at the London Palladium* where they meet Alma Cogan.

January 14 The Beatles fly to Paris to appear at Olympia Theatre for a three week engagement, the first night of which was January 17.

January 20 US album release *Meet The Beatles* on Capitol ST2047.

January 27 US single release of *My Bonnie/The Saints* as Tony Sheridan & The Beatles on MGM K13213.

January 29 The Beatles record German language versions of *She Loves You* and *I Want to Hold Your Hand* in Paris.

January 30 US single release of *Please, Please Me/From Me to You* on Vee Jay VJ581.

February 1 *I Want To Hold Your Hand* makes No.1 on the US charts.

February 5 The Beatles arrive home from Paris.

February 7 UK EP release *All My Loving* on Parlophone GEP 8891. The Beatles leave London's Heathrow airport onboard a PanAm Boeing 707 for New York's JFK Airport where on arrival they hold a press conference.

February 8 A press call in New York's Central Park, which did not include George as he was feeling unwell, was followed by a rehearsal for *The Ed Sullivan Show*, again without George.

February 9 The Beatles rehearse for the 8 pm *Ed Sullivan Show* that is to be broadcast live that evening. They also record a segment for another *Ed Sullivan Show* broadcast on 23 February.

February 11 The Beatles take the train to Washington DC because a snowstorm had hit the East Coast. They play The Washington Coliseum (their first concert in the US) that evening and attend a cocktail party at the British Embassy.

February 12 The Beatles take the train back to New York City before playing two shows at Carnegie Hall.

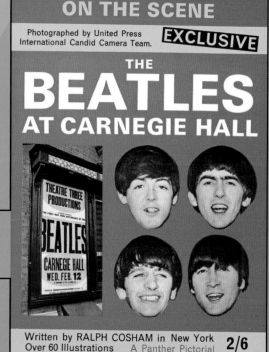

February 13 The Beatles fly to Miami.

February 14 Rehearsal for *The Ed Sullivan Show*.

February 15 Dress rehearsal for *The Ed Sullivan Show*.

February 16   *The Ed Sullivan Show* is broadcast live to 70 million Americans.

February 21   *She Loves You* makes No.1 on the US charts. The Beatles fly home to London, arriving the following morning.

February 23   The Beatles tape an appearance on Big Night Out TV show.

February 25   George's 21st birthday and the Beatles finish recording *Can't Buy Me Love* at Abbey Road.

March 2   The Beatles begin filming *A Hard Day's Night*, which took place during most days in March. US single release *Twist And Shout/There's A Place* on Tollie 9001.

March 5   German single release *Komm Gib Mir Deine Hand/Sie Liebt Dich* on Odeon 22671.

March 16   US single release *Can't Buy Me Love/You Can't Do That* on Capitol 5150.

March 20   UK single release *Can't Buy Me Love/You Can't Do That* on Parlophone R 5114.

April 4   *Can't Buy Me Love* spends the first of its three weeks at No.1.

April 10   US album release *The Beatles Second Album* on Capitol ST 2080.

April 16   At Abbey Road recording *A Hard Day's Night*.

April 24   The last day of filming *A Hard Day's Night* that had taken place most days in April.

April 26   The Beatles top the bill at the NME Poll Winner's Concert.

April 27   US single release *Love Me Do/P.S. I Love You* on TOLLIE 9008.

April 29   Concerts at the ABC Cinema, Edinburgh and again the following evening at the Odeon Cinema in Glasgow.

May 2   John & Cynthia and George and Patti Boyd fly to Honolulu and then on to Tahiti on holiday. The following day Paul and Jane Asher and Ringo and Maureen fly to the Caribbean.

May 11   US EP release *Four by The Beatles* on Capitol EAP 2121.

May 26   John and George return from holiday; Paul and Ringo the following day.

May 30   *Love Me Do* makes No.1 on the US charts.

May 31   A Brian Epstein promoted 'Pops Alive' concert at the Prince of Wales theatre in London.

June 1   Beatles recording songs for *A Hard Day's Night* album at Abbey Road.

June 3   Ringo collapses with tonsillitis and is taken to hospital and ordered to rest.

June 4   The Beatles, with stand-in drummer Jimmy Nicol, fly to Denmark to begin a world tour.

June 5   Concert in Amsterdam, followed by another the next day in Blokker.

June 7   The Beatles with Jimmy fly to Hong Kong and play a concert on June 9.

June 10   The Beatles fly to Australia.

June 12   Ringo leaves London to fly to Australia via San Francisco and the band plays a concert in Adelaide and again the following evening.

June 15   The Beatles play Melbourne, Australia with Ringo back on the drums and again the following two evenings.

June 18   The Beatles play Sydney, Australia and again on June 20. UK EP release *Long Tall Sally* on Parlophone GEP 8913.

June 21   The Beatles arrive in New Zealand.

June 22   Concert in Wellington, NZ, and the following evening.

June 24   Concert in Auckland, NZ, and the following evening.

June 26   US album release *A Hard Day's Night* on United Artists UAS 6366. Concert in Dunedin, NZ.

June 27   Concert in Christchurch, NZ.

June 29   Concert in Brisbane, Australia and the following evening.

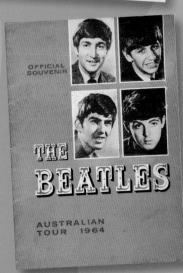

July 2   The Beatles arrive home from Australia and later in the day Paul plays piano on Cilla Black's *It's For You* at Abbey Road watched by John.

July 6   Premiere of *A Hard Day's Night* in London.

July 10   The Beatles fly from London to Liverpool for the Northern premiere of *A Hard Day's Night* in Liverpool. UK single release *A Hard Day's Night/Things We Said Today* on Parlophone R 5160 and UK album release for *A Hard Day's Night* on Parlophone PCS 3058.

July 12   Concert at the Hippodrome in Brighton.

July 13   US single release *A Hard Day's Night/I Should Have Known Better* on Capitol 5222.

July 20   US single releases *I'll Cry Instead/I'm Happy Just To Dance With You* on Capitol 5234 and *And I Love Her/If I Fell* on Capitol 5235. US album release *Somethng New* on Capitol ST 2108.

July 25   A *Hard Day's Night* gets to No.1, the first of three weeks at the top of the charts.

July 26   Concert at the Opera House, Blackpool.

July 29   Concert in Stockholm, Sweden having flown there the previous day.

August 1   A *Hard Day's Night* makes No.1 on the US charts.

August 2   Concert at the Gaumont Cinema in Bournemouth.

August 9   Concert at the Futurist Theatre in Scarborough.

August 11   The Beatles start work on the *Beatles For Sale* album at Abbey Road.

August 12   A *Hard Day's Night* premieres in cities across America.

August 16   Concert at the Opera House in Blackpool.

August 18   The Beatles leave London to begin their 25 date tour of the US and Canada.

August 19   The first show of the tour at the Cow Palace in San Francisco.

August 24   US single release *Slow Down/Matchbox* on Capitol 5255.

September 20   The last night of the US tour is at the Paramount Theatre on Broadway in New York City.

September 21   The Beatles arrive at Heathrow Airport at 9.30 pm where they are greeted by thousands of fans.

September 29   Back in the studio at Abbey Road working on *Beatles For Sale* album.

October 3   Recording Jack Good's *Shindig!* for American TV live before a studio audience in London.

October 9   The first night of a month long UK tour opens at the Gaumont Cinema in Bradford.

November 4   UK EP release A *Hard Day's Night* on Parlophone GEP 8920.

November 10   The final night of their UK tour is at Colston Hall, Bristol.

November 23   The Beatles record a TV appearance on *Ready Steady Go!*.

November 27   UK single release *I Feel Fine/She's A Woman* on Parlophone R 5200.

December 1   Ringo enters hospital to have his tonsils removed.

December 4   UK album release *Beatles For Sale* on Parlophone PCS 3062.

December 12   *I Feel Fine* tops the UK chart for the first of its 5 weeks at No.1.

December 15   US album release *Beatles '65* on Capitol ST 2228.

December 21   Rehearsals begin for *Another Beatles Christmas Show* at the Hammersmith Odeon in London.

December 24   Opening night of *Another Beatles Christmas Show*.

December 26   *I feel Fine* makes No.1 on the US charts.

ABOVE: *Backstage with French singing star, Sylvie Vartan, who had the difficult job of appearing immediately before the Beatles during the show.*

En Paris

John, Paul and George left London Heathrow for Paris on Tuesday 14 January and stayed at the George V hotel. Ringo followed on a day later having been fog bound in Liverpool airport. After breakfast on Wednesday morning, while waiting for Ringo to arrive the three of them took a stroll down the Champs Elysées to buy some postcards to send home. That evening they had a rehearsal along with the other French stars who were to appear alongside them on the bill at the Olympia Theatre. The show opened on Friday 17 January and ran until Tuesday 4 February.

LEFT: *Outside the Olympia Theatre*

"The crowd was a lot different from the ones we're used to in England. The ones in England are mostly girls – here mostly boys. When they yell it is more like a cheer rather than a squeal."

RINGO IN PARIS AFTER THEIR FIRST SHOW

Leaving on a jet plane

After just two days at home the Beatles were off again, this time for their first visit to America. Cynthia Lennon went with John on what was to be the most important few weeks in the band's career. The Beatles at London's Heathrow Airport prior to their departure onboard PanAm flight 101.

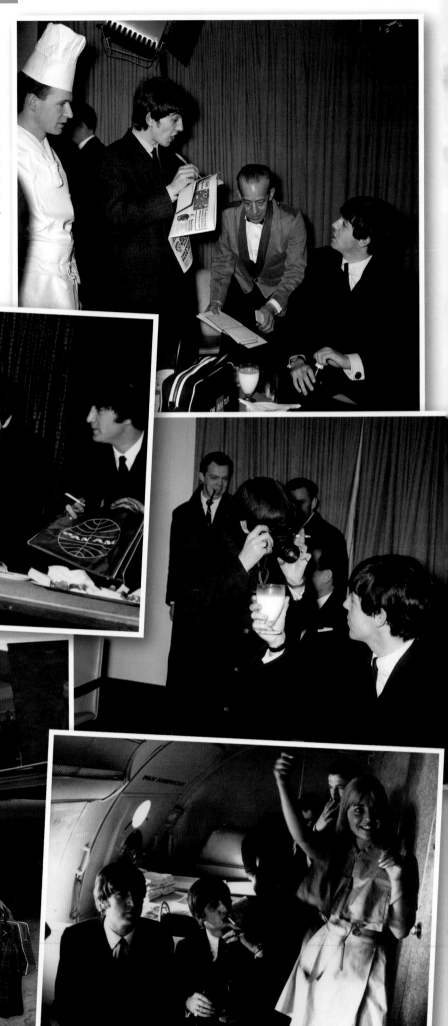

Will you sing something?'
JOURNALIST

"No."
JOHN

"Can you sing?"
JOURNALIST

"Not without money."
JOHN

"How much money do you expect to make in the USA?"
JOURNALIST

"About half a crown."
GEORGE

Meet The Beatles

Having arrived from London the previous day all four Beatles were scheduled to do a press photocall in New York's Central Park prior to attending rehearsals for *The Ed Sullivan Show* on the morning of February 8. George had a bad throat so he made neither the photo call nor the rehearsal. Neil Aspinall stood in for George in what was principally a TV camera call, followed by a chance for the press to once again, meet the Beatles. Before it was over George arrived for a full Fab Four photocall.

The Ed Sullivan Show

The Beatles played live on the show on February 9 and 16.

Meet The Press

Before the band left for Washington there was a press conference at which Capital's President, Alan Livingstone, the man who signed them to the label, gave them a gold record for a million copies of *I Want To Hold Your Hand* and another for a million dollars worth of sales for their LP, *Meet The Beatles*. In Washington the band attended a press conference at the Washington Coliseum before their appearance. The concert was 'in the round', which meant between numbers Ringo's kit had to be moved around as they faced different sections of the audience.

The Ambassador's Do

The band gave a press conference in the late afternoon of 11 February to the assembled Press corps at the Washington Coliseum and in the evening played a 12-song set to a crowd of 8,000 fans, mostly screaming girls. Also on the bill were the Chiffons and Tommy Roe. After the concert the band went to the British Embassy for a reception hosted by the Ambassador, Lord Ormsby-Gore. It was at the party that Ringo had a small lock of his hair cut off by one of the guests – he was not pleased. John was also upset by the attention he received and he and the band apparently told Brian Epstein never to get them involved in such an event again. In the top picture the Ambassador introduces the Beatles, John is clearly not impressed; below, Paul is obviously doing his bit at promoting the band.

From Washington to New York City by Train

Having taken the train to Washington from New York City the party returned the same way on 12 February. John is seen talking to New York DJ, Murray the K.

ABOVE: *Back in New York City the band played two back to back shows at Carnegie Hall*

Miami

The Beatles flew south to Miami on 13 February and checked into the Deauville Hotel on Miami Beach. They were there to film another appearance on *The Ed Sullivan Show* and besides rehearsing for their appearance they managed to grab some sun and meet some girls on the Beach. Their TV appearance was transmitted on 16 February and after a few days spent relaxing in the sun they flew home to London.

"We should last longer, we don't drink."

PAUL WHEN ASKED IF THE BEATLES WOULD LAST LONGER THAN FRANK SINATRA

21 today!

Three days after arriving at London airport the band were at Abbey Road to record and it was also George's 21st birthday. He received over 50 sacks of mail, some of which went to his parents' home in Liverpool (Mr & Mrs Harrison met the postmen at the door), the rest to the Beatles Fan Club in London's Monmouth Street; the secretary of the fan club Anne Collingham (left) had her work cut out dealing with it all.

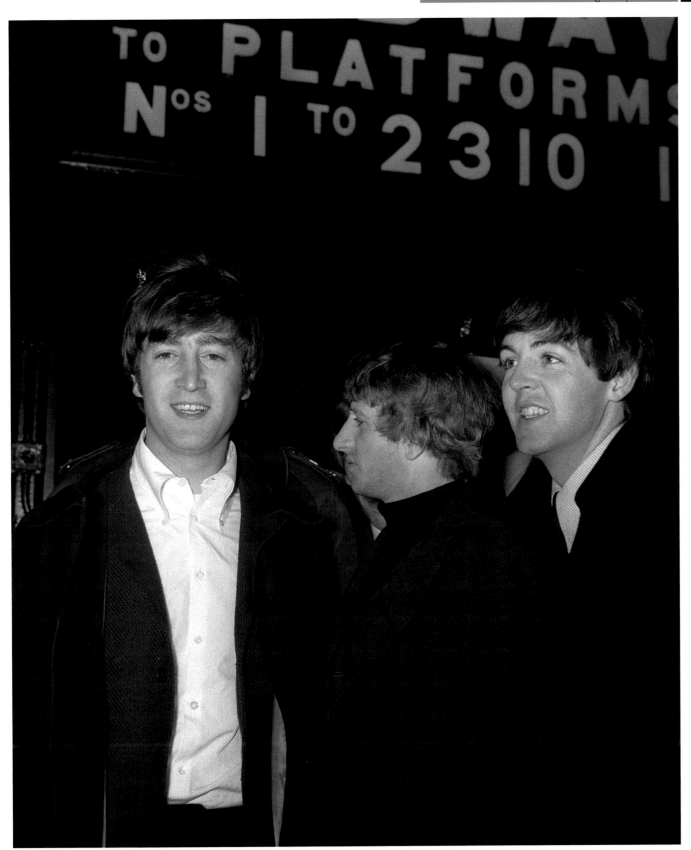

ABOVE: *Leaving London's Paddington Station on 5 March to take the train to Minehead.*

A Hard Day's Night

Filming on the Beatles first movie started on 2 March and continued for most days during the month and up until 24 April. It included location filming in Minehead in Somerset, which involved additional scenes being shot on a train journey. Much of the interior scenes were done in Twickenham Film Studios, with some scenes filmed around the local area. A concert sequence was filmed at the end of the month at the Scala Theatre in London's Charlotte Street.

The Eyes Have it

While they were filming at Twickenham Film Studios, Madame Tussauds technicians arrived to make sure the Beatles' eyes for their waxwork dummies matched perfectly.

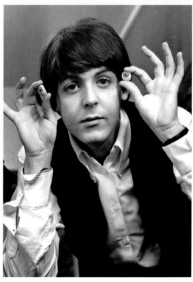

The Scala
Theatre

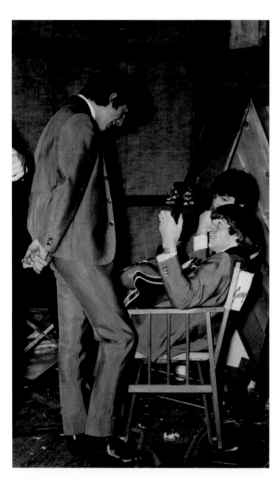

The Weekend Starts Here!

Ready Steady Go!, the best music show during the 1960s, hosted by Cathy McGowan, featured the Beatles on the programme during the filming of *A Hard Day's Night*. On 20 March they mimed to *Can't Buy Me Love, You Can't Do That* and *It Won't Be Long*; it was their second appearance on the show that opened with the immortal words, the weekend starts here – it was broadcast throughout most of Britain on a Friday night, although in some regions it was on different nights, which probably confused a few people! All these pictures were taken during the rehearsals for the live show.

Busy Boys

With filming over the pace of work did not let up, it just altered. As filming was finishing John went to the launch of his book, *In His Own Write*, on 23 April and in the evening he and Ringo went to Roy Orbison's 28th birthday party. Then there were rehearsals for the band's first TV spectacular started on 25 April, *Around The Beatles* (it was taped on 28 April and aired on 6 May), the band topped the bill at the annual NME Poll Winners' Concert at the Empire Pool Wembley on 26 April, found time for a photo shoot at Madame Tussauds with their waxwork dummies and on 29 and 30 April there were two shows a night on each date, in Glasgow and Edinburgh. On 2 May the band all went on holiday.

Around The Beatles

LEFT AND BELOW: *At the NME Poll winners' concert and the real thing and their dummies.*

New Drummer Jimmy.

Back from holiday at the end of May, with *Love Me Do* at No.1 on the US charts, they played a Brian Epstein promoted 'Pops Alive' concert at the Prince of Wales theatre in London. The following day they were in the studio recording songs for *A Hard Day's Night* album when Ringo collapsed with tonsillitis – he was taken to hospital and ordered to rest. This was a problem as the band were off on tour, starting out in Denmark on 4 June and ending up in New Zealand by the end of June. The solution to their immediate problem was to hire a stand-in drummer – which is how Jimmy Nicol was flying with the other three Beatles to Copenhagen to begin their tour.

Film Night

Four days after getting home from the lands down under the premiere of *A Hard Day's Night* took place at the London Pavilion. Piccadilly Circus in London came to a standstill.

The Prodigals Return

The Beatles flew home to Liverpool on 10 July for the Northern premiere of *A Hard Day's Night*. The scenes in the city were unprecedented. Everyone wanted to see, and probably touch the city's favourite sons. After arriving at Liverpool's Speke airport accompanied by a gaggle of pressmen and the DJ, David Jacobs, they gave a press conference before heading into the city centre in a cavalcade. After a reception in the Town Hall with the Mayor it was off to the premiere at the Odeon Cinema.

Oh, I do like to be beside the seaside

The tradition of seaside holidays during the summer in Britain had given rise to summer variety shows at British resorts and the Beatles, like every other entertainer joined in the fun. There were concerts in Blackpool, Bournemouth, Brighton and just to prove that not all resorts begin with 'B' there was one at Scarborough. The band also appeared on Mike and Bernie Winters' *Blackpool Night Out* filmed in Blackpool, with co-star Chita Rivera (both the colour shots). In Scarborough the Beatles appeared with singer Cherry Rowland.

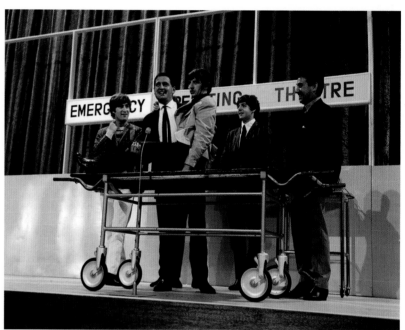

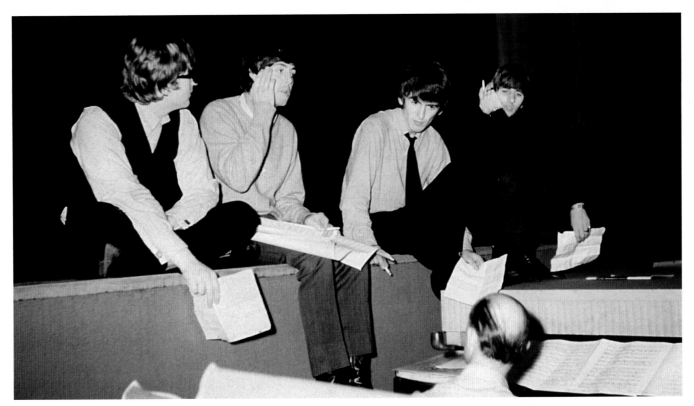

The Night of a Thousand Stars

Doing their bit for charity they took part in a star-studded night at the London Palladium on 23 July in aid of the Combined Theatrical Charities Appeal Council. They agreed to do an 'aerial ballet' sequence as well as play a couple of songs. Among the other stars were Zsa Zsa Gabor (seen with Paul), Judy Garland, Sir Laurence Olivier and Jane Asher.

ABOVE: *Leaving London's Heathrow Airport.*

ABOVE: *Arriving at San Francisco shortly before 7 p.m.*

ABOVE: *Greeting fans from a specially constructed platform.*

ABOVE: *The litter left at San Francisco Airport by the fans.*

From Sea to Shining Sea

On 18 August the band left London for their 25 date tour of North America. They flew via Winnipeg in Canada where around 500 fans were at the airport to wave hello. In Los Angeles, where they landed next, 2,000 fans had gathered and by the time they got to San Francisco for the first date on the tour, the very next day, 9,000 hysterical fans were there to greet them.

We Saw Them Standing There

On every night of the tour the same scenes were played out across America. The pictures (opposite) were from the opening show at San Francisco's Cow Palace on 19 August while those below (and on the following two pages) were from the following night inside Las Vegas' 8,000-seat Convention Center. Each night they played *Twist and Shout, You Can't Do That, All My Loving, She Loves You, Things We Said Today, Roll Over Beethoven, Can't Buy me Love, If I Fell, I Want To Hold Your Hand, A Hard Day's Night* and *Long Tall Sally* as the closer. Sometimes they would start with *I Saw Her Standing There* and closed with *Twist and Shout.* . .not that too many people heard very much.

Time To Themselves

The opportunities to relax on the tour were few and far between, if The Beatles were not performing they were usually travelling or attending a press call. The pictures of Ringo with gun and holster along with John and Paul on horseback were taken at a Missouri ranch on 19 September. The others were taken at a rented house in Bel Air, Los Angeles.

ABOVE: *With Dean Martin's daughter Claudia at a garden party in Los Angeles on the 23 August*

Forest Hills Tennis Stadium

Almost 16,000 fans watched The Beatles play their set at a stadium more used to tennis than pop. With tickets priced at $6.50, the equivalent of $50 today they were treated to a typical Beatles' set that included – *Roll Over Beethoven, Can't Buy Me Love, If I Fell, A Hard Day's Night* and *All My Loving*. The band flew into Forest Hills by helicopter and flew out again, but they still had to get to and from the stage!

No Let Up

Home from their gruelling US tour the band were back in the studio a week later working on tracks for their *Beatles For Sale* album, which continued intermittently for the next week. Following the shooting of an appearance on Jack Good's American TV series, *Shindig!*, that was filmed in Fulham on 3 October, the band were back on stage at the Gaumont in Bradford on 9 October, John Lennon's 24th birthday, for the start of a British tour that continued until 10 November. The main support act was the former Motown star, Mary Wells.

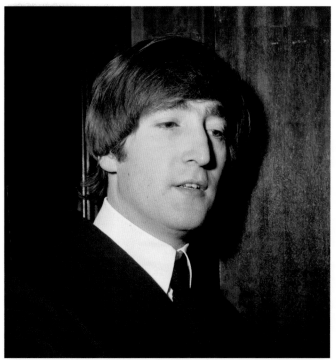

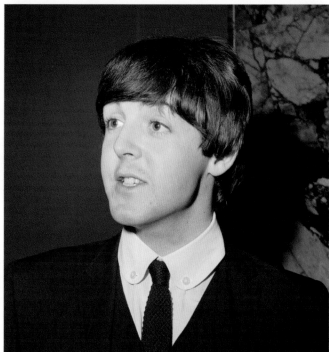

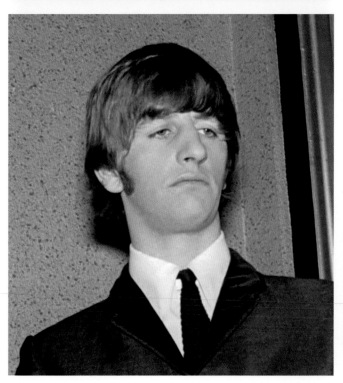

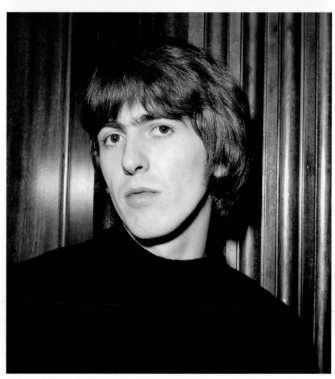

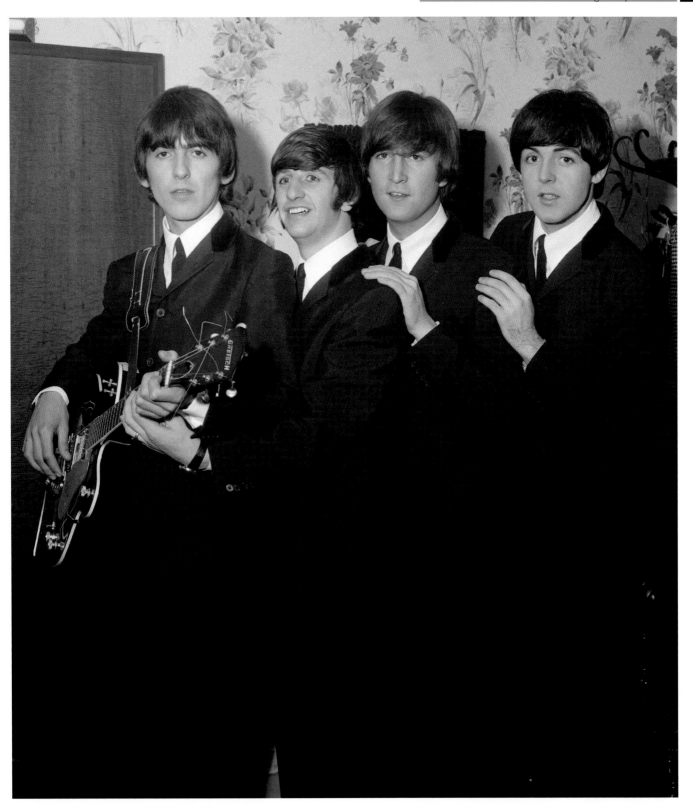

*"We knew America
would make us or
break us as world stars.
In fact, she made us."*

BRIAN EPSTEIN

SUNDAY NOV. 10TH
THE BEATLES
ALL SEATS & STANDING
ROOM COMPLETELY
SOLD OUT

In...

On 1 December Ringo went into University College Hospital, London, to have his tonsils removed.

...and Out

He came out on 10 December with them gone. He's seen flanked by Beatles assistants Alistair Taylor (left) and driver Alf Bicknell (right).

Another Beatles Christmas Show

Four days before Christmas the band began rehearsals for their holiday show at the Hammersmith Odeon. It ran twice nightly from Christmas Eve until Saturday 16 January. John, Paul, George and Ringo performed a sketch together with Freddie (of the Dreamers) and DJ Jimmy Saville. On page 158/9 the majority of the cast is seen assembled on stage for a photocall. Peering out from the back, just above Ringo is Eric Clapton who was with the Yardbirds. Elkie Brooks is surrounded by members of the Mike Cotton Sound and Freddie and the Dreamers grouped behind Paul and George.

BRIAN EPSTEIN Presents

ANOTHER BEATLES CHRISTMAS SHOW

The MIKE COTTON SOUND	The MIKE COTTON SOUND
MICHAEL HASLAM	ELKIE BROOKS
The YARDBIRDS	SOUNDS INCORPORATED
JIMMY SAVILE	RAY FELL
FREDDIE and the DREAMERS	JIMMY SAVILE
	THE BEATLES

INTERVAL

DEVISED AND PRODUCED BY PETER YOLLAND

1965

So Self Assured

THERE WAS A NOTICEABLE slackening in the pace of work for a band that had spent the last four years working harder than any other group in Britain. The Beatles began filming *Help!* in February, which took longer than *A Hard Day's Night*, with location work in the Bahamas and Austria. A third US tour is massive with The Beatles setting a new record when they play to over 55,000 people at New York's Shea Stadium. A series of UK concerts in December will become their last tour of Britain. And all through the year the hits just keep on coming.

1965 TIMELINE

January 1   The Beatles continue their holiday show at the Hammersmith Odeon. *I Feel Fine* stays at No.1 for the first two weeks of the year on the UK singles' chart.

January 16   The last night of *Another Beatles Christmas Show*.

January 25   John and Cynthia join George Martin and his future wife on a skiing holiday in St Moritz; George and Patti visit Europe, while Paul and Jane go away on holiday to Tunisia.

February 11   Ringo marries Maureen Cox at Caxton Hall in London giving a press conference in the Beatles' solicitor's garden the following day.

February 15   US single release *Eight Days a Week/I Don't Want To Spoil The Party* on Capitol 5371. John passes his driving test.

February 16   Sessions for the *Help!* soundtrack album running until February 20.

February 21   A specially charted BOAC Boeing 707 leaves Heathrow for the Bahamas where the filming of *Help!* was to commence.

February 22   Filming *Help!* starts, although at this point it had the working title, *Eight Arms To Hold You*.

March 11   The Beatles arrive back in London from the Bahamas.

March 13   The Beatles leave Heathrow to fly to Salzburg in Austria for more filming. *Eight Days A Week* tops the *Billboard* chart for the first of its two weeks.

March 22   The Beatles return from Austria.

March 24   Filming commences at Twickenham Studios.

April 3   The Beatles appear on *Thank Your Lucky Stars*, which was recorded on March 28; it's their first TV appearance of the year.

April 6   UK EP release *Beatles For Sale*, on Parlophone GEP 8931 that includes, *No Reply, I'm A Loser, Rock And Roll Music* and *Eight Days A Week*.

April 9   UK Single release *Ticket To Ride/Yes It Is* on Parlophone R5265.

1	**I FEEL FINE**
	1 (6) The Beatles (Parlophone)
2	**YEH, YEH**
	7 (4) Georgie Fame (Columbia)
3	**DOWNTOWN**
	2 (9) Petula Clark (Pye)
4	**TERRY**
	10 (7) Twinkle (Decca)
5	**WALK TALL**
	3 (13) Val Doonican (Decca)
6	**I'M GONNA BE STRONG**
	4 (9) Gene Pitney (Stateside)
7	**GIRL DON'T COME**
	11 (5) Sandie Shaw (Pye)
8	**SOMEWHERE**
	9 (5) P. J. Proby (Liberty)
9	**I COULD EASILY FALL**
	6 (5) Cliff Richard (Columbia)
10	**GO NOW!**
	19 (5) Moodyblues (Decca)

ODEON HAMMERSMITH Tel: RIV 4081

ON THE STAGE

BRIAN EPSTEIN Presents

ANOTHER 'BEATLES' CHRISTMAS SHOW

THE BEATLES

FREDDIE and the DREAMERS

JIMMY SAVILE · SOUNDS INCORPORATED

ELKIE BROOKS · THE YARDBIRDS · MICHAEL HASLAM
THE MIKE COTTON SOUND · RAY FELL

OPENS 24th DECEMBER to 16th JANUARY 1965
(EXCEPT SUNDAYS)

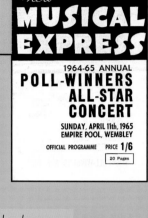

MAURICE KINN
presents the

new

MUSICAL EXPRESS

1964-65 ANNUAL
POLL-WINNERS
ALL-STAR
CONCERT

SUNDAY, APRIL 11th, 1965
EMPIRE POOL, WEMBLEY

OFFICIAL PROGRAMME   PRICE **1/6**

20 Pages

April 11   The Beatles top the bill at the NME Poll Winners concert at the Empire Pool, Wembley.

April 14   Paul buys a new home in London's St John's Wood.

April 18   The Beatles Poll Winner's appearance is featured on TV's *Big Beat '65* show.

April 19   US single release *Ticket To Ride/Yes It Is* on Capitol 5407.

April 24   The first of three weeks at No.1 in the UK for *Ticket To Ride*.

April 28   Peter Sellers presents each of the band with a Grammy for *A Hard Day's Night* during filming at Twickenham.

April 30   More filming at Twickenham, as there had been on most days during the month of April.

May 3   Filming sequences for *Help!* on Salisbury Plain with the British Army that takes three days.

May 11   The last day of filming *Help!* takes place at Clivedon House in Berkshire.

May 22   *Ticket To Ride* spends one week at the top of the Billboard chart.

May 26   The Beatles record their last show for BBC radio. It was retitled from, *From Us To You*, to *The Beatles Invite you to Take a Ticket To Ride*.

May 27   Holiday time! Paul and Jane go to Portugal where he writes the lyrics to *Yesterday* in a car from the airport to Shadows' guitarist Bruce Welch's villa where they are staying.

June 4   UK EP release *Beatles For Sale 2* on Parlophone GEP 8938 that includes *I'll Follow The Sun, Baby's In Black, Words Of Love*, and *I Don't Want To Spoil The Party*.

June 11   Paul and Jane fly back early from holiday, as Brian Epstein wanted all The Beatles to be in Britain when the announcement that they are to receive the MBE is made. The story breaks on the evening news, which causes consternation for some and deep joy for others...including the Beatles.

June 14   Paul records *Yesterday*.

June 20   The Beatles begin a short European tour with a show at the Palais des Sports in Paris.

July 4   Arriving at Heathrow there are the usual crowds but not as large as in recent times. The tour had taken in, Lyons, Milan, Genoa, Rome, Nice, Madrid, and Barcelona

July 19   US single release, *Help! I'm Down* on Capitol 5476. Ringo buys Sunny Heights in Weybridge.

July 23   UK single release, *Help! I'm Down* on Parlophone R 5305.

July 29   The premiere of *Help!* at the London Pavilion cinema. 10,000 fans turn out.

August 1   The band appear on *Blackpool Night Out* hosted by Mike and Bernie Winters, along with Pearl Carr and Teddy Johnson and dancer Lionel Blair.

August 6   UK album release. *Help!* on Parlophone PMC 1255 (mono) & PCS 3071 (stereo).

August 7   The first of three weeks at No.1 for *Help!* on the UK singles' chart.

August 11   *Help!* opens in New York.

August 13   US album release. *Help!* on Capitol MAS-2386 (mono) & SMAS-2386 (stereo). The band arrive in New York for their third US tour.

August 15   Their record-breaking performance at New York's Shea Stadium in front of a crowd of 55,600. Dates follow in Toronto, Atlanta, Houston, Chicago, Minneapolis, Portland, San Diego, Los Angeles and San Francisco.

September 2   The Beatles arrive back in London.

September 4   *Help!* spends the first of its three weeks at the top of the Billboard singles' chart.

September 13 US single release, *Yesterday/Act Naturally* on Capitol 5498. Maureen and Ringo's son, Zak, the future drummer for The Who, is born.

October 9   *Yesterday* spends the first of four weeks at No.1 on the Billboard chart.

October 11   Marianne Faithfull records *Yesterday*, but her version loses out on the charts to Matt Monro's rendition.

October 16   *Day Tripper* is recorded at Abbey Road. Before the month is out they will have recorded *Nowhere Man, We Can Work It Out, Norwegian Wood* and *I'm looking Through You.*

October 26   The Beatles go to Buckingham Palace to receive their MBEs from Her Majesty The Queen.

November 1 The band start work on a TV special, *The Music Of Lennon & McCartney* at Granada TV in Manchester; they finish work the next day.

November 3 *Michelle* is recorded at Abbey Road.

December 3 UK single release *Day Tripper/We Can Work It Out* on Parlophone R5389. UK album release, *Rubber Soul* on Parlophone PMC 1267 (mono) and PCS 30765 (stereo). The opening night of the Beatles very last UK tour kicks off at Glasgow's Odeon Cinema.

December 4 The City Hall, Newcastle.

December 5 Liverpool Empire.

December 6 US album release, *Rubber Soul* on Capitol T 2442 (mono) and ST 2442 (stereo).

December 7 ABC Cinema in Ardwick, Manchester.

December 8 Gaumont Cinema, Bradford.

December 9 The Odeon Cinema, Birmingham.

December 10 London's Hammersmith, Odeon.

December 11 London's Finsbury Park, Astoria.

December 12 Cardiff Capitol Cinema; the last date of their final British concert tour.

December 16 *The Music Of Lennon & McCartney* show airs on Granada Television.

December 18 The first of five weeks at No.1 on the UK singles' chart for *Day Tripper/We Can Work it Out.*

St. Moritz

On 25 January John and Cynthia flew to
Switzerland before transferring to St Moritz to join
George Martin and his wife-to-be, Judy Lockhart-
Smith on a skiing holiday; George injured his leg
and so he hardly skied at all.

Mrs Starkey

Ringo proposed to Maureen Cox at the end of December and the couple got married at Caxton Hall in London on 11 February; John, George and Brian Epstein, who was best man, all attended, but Paul was away on holiday in Tunisia. The following day the couple 'meet the press' in the garden of the band's solicitor, David Jacobs in Hove, Sussex.

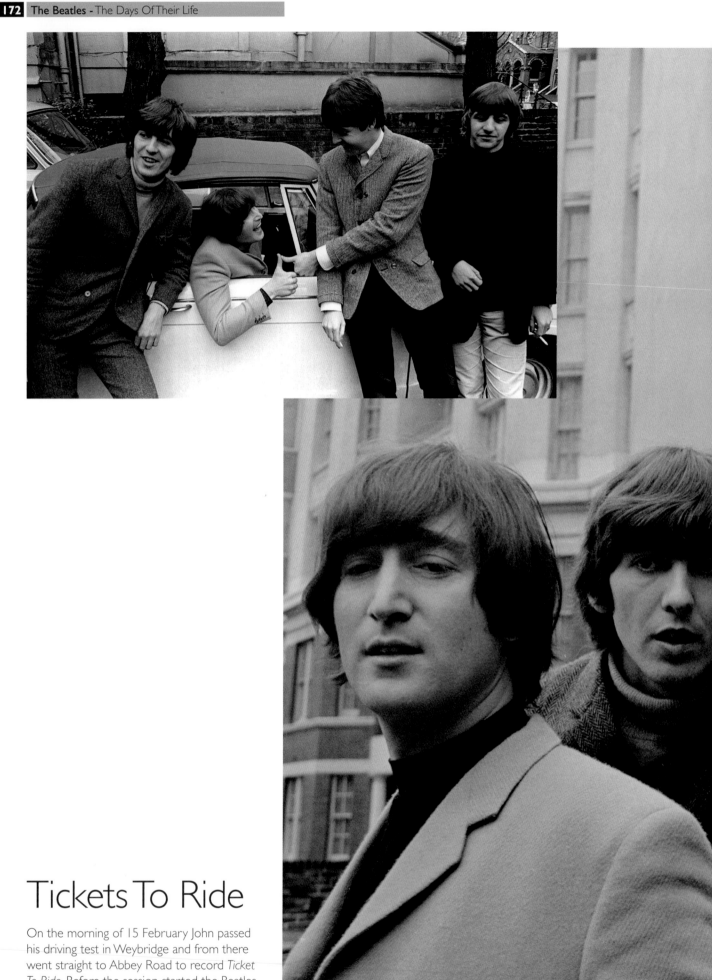

Tickets To Ride

On the morning of 15 February John passed his driving test in Weybridge and from there went straight to Abbey Road to record *Ticket To Ride*. Before the session started the Beatles came out so that John could be photographed in George Martin's convertible Triumph Herald.

Help!

On 22 February the Beatles, along with their co-star Eleanor Bron, other cast members and crew, left chilly London for the Bahamas on a specially chartered Boeing 707 to begin filming *Help!* On 11 March they arrived back in London and two days later they flew to Austria for 10 more days of location filming. Two days after flying back from Salzburg they began shooting at Twickenham Studios, the surrounding area and in London: filming lasts until the end of April.

"The Beatles' road managers Neil Aspinall and Malcolm Evans were there, suitably equipped with the usual stack of photos, throat sweets, ciggies and other essential Beatle touring gear."

BRIAN EPSTEIN

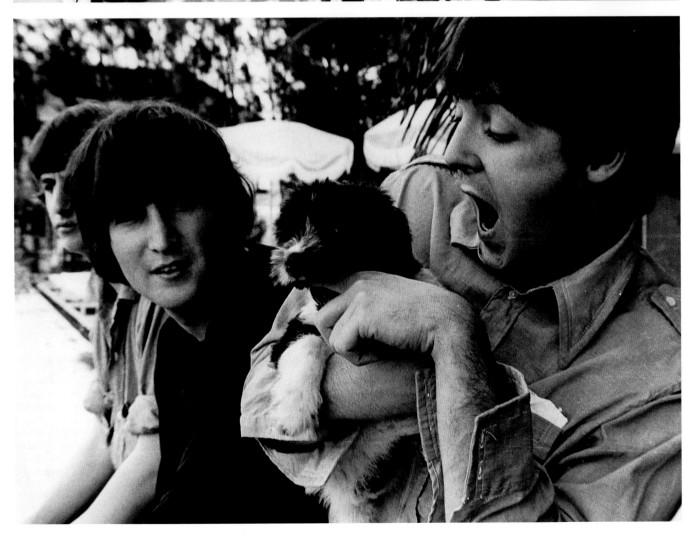

Poll Winners...Again

In the annual *New Musical Express* Awards the Beatles once again swept the board and for the third year running they topped the bill at the winners' concert at the Empire Pool, Wembley. Also appearing were (first half) The Moody Blues, Freddie & The Dreamers, Georgie Fame, Twinkle, The Seekers, Herman's Hermits, The Ivy League, Sounds Incorporated, The Bachelors, Wayne Fontana & The Mindbenders, The Rolling Stones. Then, after the Interval, The Rockin' Berries, Cilla Black, Donovan, Them, Tom Jones, The Searchers, Dusty Springfield, The Animals, with The Beatles closing the show. They played *I Feel Fine* (which is what they are playing in the main photograph), *She's a Woman, Baby's in Black, Ticket to Ride* and *Long Tall Sally*.

Help! is on the way

On May 3 the Beatles along with fellow cast members Eleanor Bron, Roy Kinnear, Leo McKern and Victor Spinetti joined the men and tanks of the Third Armoured Division on desolate Salisbury Plain to film a sequence for *Help!*

Members of the British Empire

Brian Epstein and the Beatles had some advance warning of the band being awarded their MBE's in the Queen's Birthday Honours list and so Brian wanted Paul back from holiday when the news broke on 11 June. The following day the band held a press conference at Twickenham Film Studios where they faced the usual phalanx of pressmen.

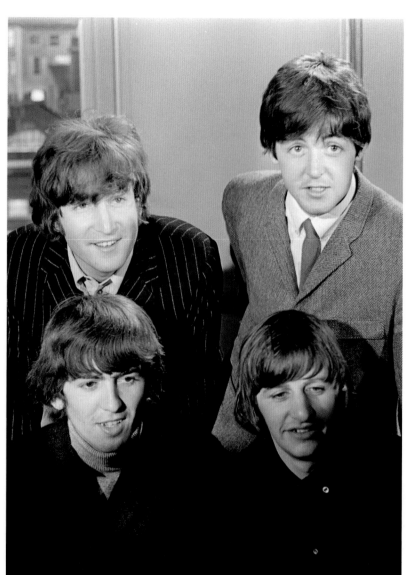

The Days After *Yesterday*

On the evening of 14 June Paul, with no help from any of the other Beatles, recorded two takes of *Yesterday*. Three days later it was completed with the addition of a string quartet. Three days later, at 3 pm, the Beatles walked onto the stage of the Palais des Sports in Place de la Porte de Versailles in Paris to play the first of their two concerts that day, the other was at 9 p.m. From Paris it was Lyon (22 June), Milan (24 June), Genoa (25 June), Rome (27 & 28 June), Nice (30 June), Madrid (2 July), Barcelona (3 July) – the band flew home to London the following day.

When I Get Home... Bungalow George

The band's growing wealth enabled them all to buy new homes. Paul bought a house on Cavendish Avenue in London's St John's Wood, Ringo bought Sunny Heights in Weybridge, Surrey in July 1965 and George a bungalow in Esher around the same time as John bought Kenwood in Weybridge in July 1964.

Cry For *Help!*

The premiere of *Help!* at London's Pavillion cinema at Piccadilly Circus turned out to be a frantic affair, on the outside at least. Around 10,000 fans turned up and many fainted had to be treated by the medical staff having been overcome with the emotion of seeing their idols. The Beatles, along with their wives, including a heavily pregnant Maureen, took it all in their stride before being introduced to Princess Margaret (again) who was accompanied by her husband Lord Snowdon.

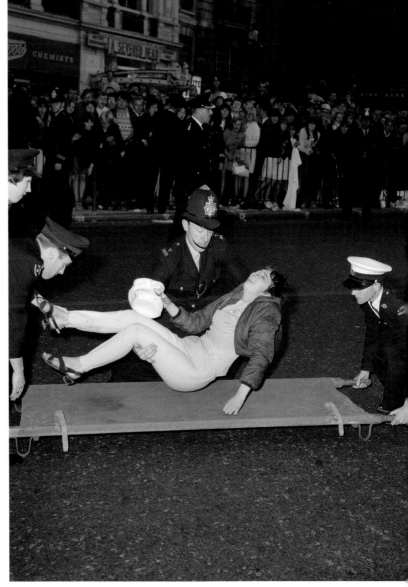

Another Night Out

On 1 August The Beatles made what was by now one of their infrequent TV appearances. It was another trip back to the seaside to appear in *Blackpool Night Out* which was hosted by Mike and Bernie Winters with other guests that included Pearl Carr and Teddy Johnson (the poor man's Mickey and Griff) and dancer Lionel Blair. It was most notable for Paul's appearance singing *Yesterday* all by himself – the first solo appearance by a Beatle. These photographs were all taken at the rehearsal during the afternoon.

"We never planned Yesterday as a solo! But John and I have written so many songs which sounded great when we sang them with one guitar and then got crummier and crummier as we added the rest of our sounds, that we decided to leave this one almost as it was."

PAUL, OCTOBER 1965

And The Band Played On...

The Beatles' second coast-to-coast tour of North America opened at Shea Stadium in New York where they wore the same suits as they had done at the NME Pollwinners concert. The idea that a band should look different from one another, when on stage, by wearing 'street clothes' was still virtually the sole preserve of the Rolling Stones and the Who. Shea Stadium set records for both the size of the audience and the takings for a single concert. The band earned a massive $160,000 out of the gross box office of $304,000 which promoter Sid Bernstein had pocketed. After New York they played Toronto, Atlanta, Houston, Chicago, Minneapolis, Portland, San Diego, Los Angeles and San Francisco.

"It would have been better still if we could have heard what we were playing. I wasn't sure what key we were in on two numbers."

JOHN

Mini Ringo & The Empire's Members

On 13 September Ringo and Maureen's son was born at Queen Charlotte's Hospital in London. They named their baby Zak. Later Zak was given his first drum kit by Keith Moon and many years later he took over the drum stool of the Who. At the end of October the Beatles went to Buckingham Palace to receive their MBE's from Her Majesty The Queen, who was, as we were later to find out, "a pretty nice girl."

The Music of Lennon and McCartney

A Granada TV special to highlight the songwriting talent of John and Paul was made on the first two days of November – it aired on 16 December. The show featured the Beatles playing *Day Tripper* and *We Can Work It Out*, which were both sides of their new single that was released in Britain on 3 December. The rest of the show was largely made up of other artists doing John and Paul's songs, including (below right from left to right): Peter and Gordon (*A World Without Love*), Marianne Faithfull (*Yesterday*), Cilla Black (*It's For You*), and Peter Sellers, who performed the hilarious Shakesperian parody of *A Hard Day's Night*.

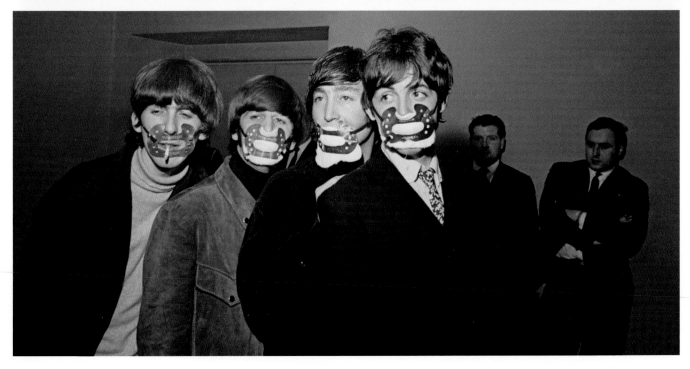

The Last British Tour

The Beatles' final British tour began at the Odeon Cinema in Glasgow on 3 December with a press conference (John using Paul's tie to wipe his nose) followed by two shows. Their set throughout the tour was *I Feel Fine, She's A Woman, If I Needed Someone, Act Naturally, Nowhere Man, Baby's In Black, Help!, We Can Work It Out, Yesterday* (Paul played it solo, while sat at an organ), *Day Tripper* and *I'm Down*. The tour finished with two shows at Cardiff's Capitol Cinema (the picture overleaf of the band with the doll was taken there) on 12 December.

1966

Records, Recordings and a Farewell

I T WAS A YEAR in which everything changed. Most noticeably the Beatles' recordings became far more complex and they took far longer over making them. No longer was there any rush to get The Beatles in and out of the studio. The band played their last American concert on what was their last performance in front of a paying audience. There were new challenges, new areas of interest to explore. The Beatles were reaching out on all sides to acting, Indian music, the arts, drugs, the counter culture ... to just about everything and anything.

1966 TIMELINE

January 1   *Rubber Soul* enters the *Billboard* album chart.

January 5   The Beatles re-record sections of the Shea Stadium concert for the film of the event and in the evening John and Cynthia went to a party at P J Proby's house.

January 8   *Rubber Soul* tops the *Billboard* album chart and *We Can Work It Out* goes to No.1 on the *Billboard* singles chart, where it spends three weeks.

January 21   George marries Pattie Boyd at the Leatherhead and Esher Register Office, before flying to Trinidad on honeymoon.

February 3   Paul goes to see Stevie Wonder play a club date in London.

February 21   US single release *Nowhere Man/What Goes On*, on Capitol 5587.

February 28   The Cavern closes with debts of £10,000 (£160,000/$210,00 today).

March 1   *The Beatles At Shea Stadium* premieres on BBC TV; it's in black and white, although it was shot in colour.

March 4   John Lennon's infamous interview in which he suggested that The Beatles might be more popular than Jesus that subsequently upset many American Christian fundamentalists.

March 24   All four Beatles attend the premiere of the film *Alfie* co-starring Jane Asher.

April 1   Paul and John visit the Indica Gallery and bookshop in Mason's Yard and among the books John buys is *The Tibetan Book of the Dead*.

April 6   The band start recording *Tomorrow Never Knows* which has as its first line words taken from *The Tibetan Book of the Dead*. For the rest of the month the band work on the tracks for *Revolver*.

April 28   The Beatles work on *Eleanor Rigby*, and again the following day.

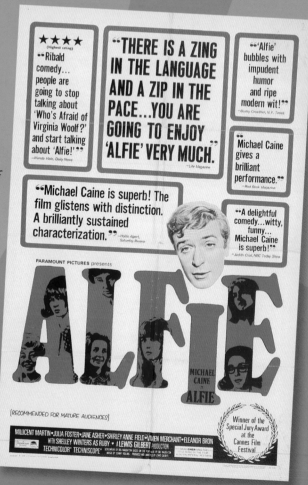

May 1   The band play the NME Pollwinners Concert at the Empire Pool, Wembley – their last ever British concert.

May 5   Back at Abbey Road continued working on tracks for *Revolver* until May 26, which is when they started work on the backing track for *Yellow Submarine*.

May 27   Paul met up with Bob Dylan and later went to his concert at the Royal Albert Hall. Over the following two days all the Beatles hung out with Dylan at his Mayfair hotel.

May 30   US single release, *Paperback Writer/ Rain* on Capitol 5651.

June 1   Back working at Abbey Road, which continued off and on until June 14.

June 10   UK single release *Paperback Writer/ Rain* on Parlophone R 5452.

June 15   US album release, *Yesterday ... and Today* on Capitol T-2553 (mono) ST 2553 (stereo).

June 16   The Beatles make their only live appearance on BBC TV's *Top of the Pops*; later they went to Abbey Road to work on *Here, There, Everywhere*, which they completed the following night. More sessions followed over the next 4 or 5 days.

June 23   The Beatles flew to Munich to begin a tour that opened the following night; there were also shows in Essen and Hamburg.

June 25   *Paperback Writer* spends the first of two weeks at No.1 on the Billboard chart, and does the same in Britain; the first time there is complete transatlantic synchronicity for the Beatles.

June 27   The Beatles flew back to London and then departed for Tokyo, but their Japanese Air Lines flight was diverted to Anchorage by a typhoon.

June 30   The Beatles arrive in Tokyo.

July 1   The band play the Budokan Hall in Tokyo and again the following night.

THE EMPIRE POOL AND SPORTS ARENA, WEMBLEY

MAY 1

ADMIT AT- SOUTH DOOR ENTRANCE

MAURICE KINN presents the ANNUAL
"NEW MUSICAL EXPRESS"
POLL WINNERS CONCERT
SUNDAY, MAY 1st, 1966
at 2 p.m.   Doors open 1.30 p.m.

33

ROW G SEAT 8

SOUTH GRAND TIER

CONDITION Neither Wembley Stadium Limited nor the Concert Promoters shall be under any legal liability for any injury loss or damage sustained by the ticket holder howsoever caused and admittance is at holder's sole risk.

30/-

TO BE RETAINED

July 3 The Beatles flew via Hong Kong to Manila where they played two football stadium shows the following day. Flying out of the Philippines the group met with harsh treatment from local police and officials after allegedly snubbing the First Lady, Imelda Marcos.

July 6 A stop in Delhi on their way home to London gives the band a couple of days off and a chance for them all to buy Indian instruments.

July 8 UK EP release *Nowhere Man* on Parlophone GEP 8952, tracks are *Nowhere Man, Drive My Car, Michelle* and *You Won't See Me*.

July 30 *Yesterday. . .And Today* reached No.1 on the *Billboard* album chart.

August 5 UK single release *Yellow Submarine/Eleanor Rigby* on Parlophone R 5493 and UK album release of *Revolver* on Parlophone PMC 7009 (mono) and PCS 7009 (stereo).

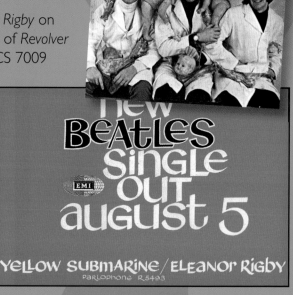

August 8 US single release *Eleanor Rigby/Yellow Submarine* on Capitol 5715 US album release *Revolver* on Capitol T-2576 (mono) & ST2576 (stereo). *Yellow Submarine* only makes No.2 on the *Billboard* chart; *Eleanor Rigby*, No.11.

August 11 The band arrives in Chicago to start their final concert tour at the International Amphitheatre the following day. Over the next 17 days they play 14 different cities.

August 20 *Yellow Submarine/Eleanor Rigby* spends the first of 4 weeks at No.1 in the UK.

August 29 The Beatles final concert takes place at Candlestick Park, San Francisco.

September 5 John flies to Hannover to begin filming *How I Won The War*.

September 10 *Revolver* tops the US album chart.

September 14 George and Patti fly to India where George is to take sitar lessons from Ravi Shankar; they stay at the Taj Mahal Hotel in Bombay.

The moment of apology—JOHN LENNON (right) says he's sorry if any religious statement made by him offended anyone. He apologised for the mistaken impression he gave, but not for holding controversial opinions. GEORGE HARRISON sits beside John at the Chicago Press conference last Thursday night.

October 22 George and Pattie return from India, George meets Ravi Shankar at Heathrow four days later when he arrives in Britain to play some concerts.

November 1 By this time John has finished filming *How I Won The War* in Spain.

November 9 John meets Yoko Ono at the Indica Gallery where she is exhibiting her art.

November 24 Back together in Abbey Road the band begin recording a new album – their first track is *Strawberry Fields Forever*, work continues on the track on November 28 & 29.

November 27 John films an appearance in Peter Cook and Dudley Moore's *Not Only... But Also* TV series.

December 6 Work continues on the new album on and off through December with Paul working on *Penny Lane* on December 29 and 30.

December 10 UK album release *A Collection Of Beatles Oldies* on Parlophone PMC 7016 (mono) and PCS 7016 (stereo).

Holiday and Honeymoon

John, Cynthia, Ringo and Maureen went on holiday to Port of Spain and were there when George and Patti were married at the Leatherhead and Esher Register Office where Brian Epstein and Paul were the best men.

What's It All About?

Apart from a little studio work the band had spent the first three months of the year enjoying themselves. Their first public outing as a foursome was to attend the premier of *Alfie* in the West End. The film starred Michael Caine and among its co-stars was Jane Asher; Cilla Black, who had a hit with the title song from the film was there too.

It's No.1 ...It's Top Of The Pops

On 16 June the Beatles made their only live appearance on the BBC's *Top of the Pops* to promote *Paperback Writer;* the following week it went to No.1.

Back In Germany

On 23 June the band flew to Munich to play three cities.
Their first date was at the Circus-Krone-Bau in Munich on the
following night where they played two shows. On the next
night it was Essen and the night after that then Ernest Merck
Halle in Hamburg. With heavy police security and motorcycle
escorts, it was all a far cry from their days playing the city's
sleazy nightclubs just five years earlier.

Far Out in the Far East

Flying home to London from Germany on 27 June the band and their entourage, including Brian Epstein, then left, almost immediately, on the first Japan Air Lines polar flight to Tokyo. Unfortunately a typhoon caused the aircraft to divert to Anchorage where there was a subsequent delay. They eventually arrived on 30 June a little before 4 a.m. They checked into the Hilton and held a press conference before playing the Budokan Hall that evening; concerts followed on the next two evenings with the band leaving Tokyo on 3 July to fly to Manila in the Philippines via Hong Kong. The band played two football stadium shows in Manila the following day. Flying out of the Philippines the group met with harsh treatment from local police and officials after allegedly snubbing the First Lady, Imelda Marcos.

PHILIPPINES
Beatles clash
with President.
Beatles row
with Taxmen.

'I thought it was the usual police escort'

"When I started playing it, it wasn't my idea to make it the 'in' instrument. I can't help it if everyone else takes up the instrument and starts playing a whole new thing in music."

GEORGE, NOVEMBER 1966

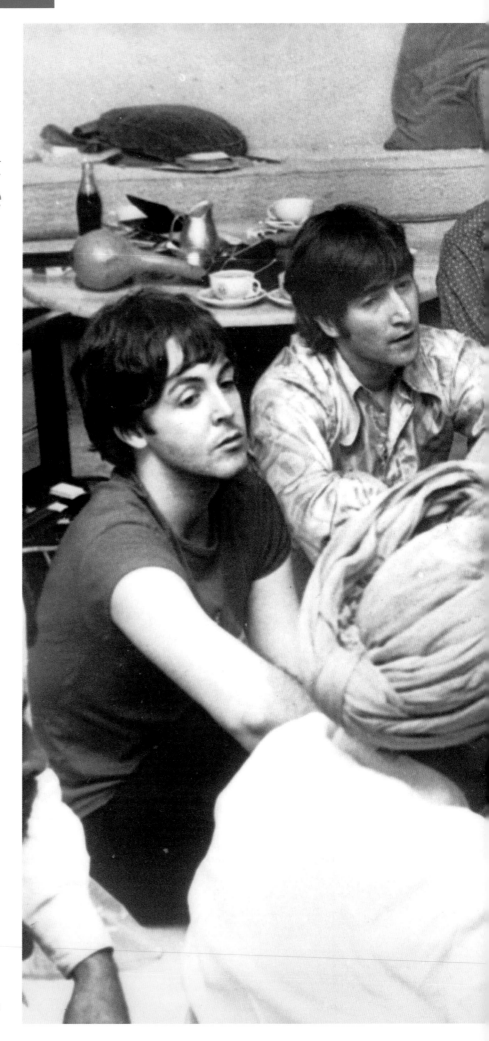

RIGHT: *On their way back to London from the thriller in Manila, the Beatles stopped in New Delhi where various Indian instruments were demonstrated for them. George Harrison was the Beatle to become most fascinated with the sounds and culture of India.*

Go West
Young Men...

A month after returning from India the Beatles
headed west on a flight from London to Chicago
to undertake what would become their last
ever concert tour. They started out in Chicago
on 12 August, played Detroit, Washington DC,
Philadelphia, Toronto, Boston, Memphis, Cincinnati,
a return to New York's Shea Stadium on 23
August (these pages), Seattle, Los Angeles and
finally (bottom photo) San Francisco's Candlestick
Park on 29 August. The following day the Beatles
flew home to London.

How He Won The War

John was at home for just a few days after finishing the American tour before he flew to Hanover to begin work on a film, *How I Won The War* with director Richard Lester, who directed both *A Hard Day's Night* and *Help!* For much of the next two months John worked on location, which included a spell in Almeria, where Clint Eastwood made most of his, so called, 'Spaghetti Westerns'. While there John composed *Strawberry Fields Forever*.

Yes!

On 9 November John met Yoko for the very first time. Yoko was putting the final touches to her exhibition at the Indica Gallery in Mason's Yard in St James's London. According to Lennon, John Dunbar, Marianne Faithfull's former husband, told him about Yoko's exhibition. John drove up from Weybridge to see it for himself and visited on the day before it opened. He was fascinated by her art, particularly the 'painting on the ceiling' that could only be viewed by climbing up a ladder to look through a magnifying glass – all it said was 'Yes'.

Not Only Pete & Dud… But Also John.

Not content with appearing in films, on 27 November John did a day's filming with comedians, Peter Cook and Dudley Moore for their *Not Only… But Also* TV series. John played a club commissionaire and is seen here with Peter Cook.

"Each one of us has, more or less, the same dilemma – What to do in the future. From time to time we gather and speak about it."

JOHN, OCTOBER 1966

1967

Sergeants Four

IT SEEMED LIKE A YEAR of almost non-stop recording – a year that included some of the Beatles most creative sessions. Career defining recordings coupled with creative ideas, some that worked, some that did not, but it all helped to redefine what a pop group could and could not do. For John, Paul, George and Ringo there were no limits and they sought inspiration from all around them; seeing many other performers in concert, reading, going to the theatre and to films, listening to different music while all the time absorbing and synthesising what they heard into their unique output. Pop music would never be the same again. . .then again is it pop music?

1967 TIMELINE

January 4   Work continues on the new Beatles' album for much of the month. On this day they worked on *Penny Lane* in particular.

January 8   John and Paul are among the guests at Georgie Fame's fancy dress party.

January 15   Paul and George see Donovan in concert and George gives Donovan sitar lessons a few days later.

January 18   Ringo and Paul go to the Bag O'Nails club in London to see the Jimi Hendrix Experience.

January 19   The Beatles start work on *A Day In The Life*.

January 27   Brian Epstein and the Beatles sign a new record deal with EMI.

January 28   George and Paul go to see the Four Tops in concert.

January 29   John and Paul go to see Jimi Hendrix, who is supporting The Who in concert at the Saville Theatre.

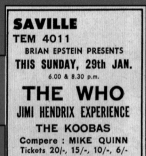

SAVILLE
TEM 4011
BRIAN EPSTEIN PRESENTS
THIS SUNDAY, 29th JAN.
6.00 & 8.30 p.m.
THE WHO
JIMI HENDRIX EXPERIENCE
THE KOOBAS
Compere : MIKE QUINN
Tickets 20/-, 15/-, 10/-, 6/-

January 31   Under pressure from EMI Brian Epstein asks George Martin for two tracks to be released as the Beatles new single. Martin reluctantly hands over *Penny Lane* and *Strawberry Fields Forever*.

February 1   The sessions for the album continue throughout the month. It started this day with work on the theme, *Sgt Pepper's Lonely Hearts Club Band*.

February 13 US single release *Penny Lane/Strawberry Fields Forever* on Capitol 5810.

February 17 UK single release *Penny Lane/Strawberry Fields Forever* on Parlophone R 5570.

February 19 John and Ringo see Chuck Berry and Del Shannon in concert at the Saville Theatre.

February 28 On the last day of the month work started on *Lucy In The Sky With Diamonds*.

March 1   Work continues on *Lucy In The Sky With Diamonds* and during the rest of the month on the album as a whole.

March 15   George and four Indian musicians recorded *Within You Without You*.

March 18   *Penny Lane* tops the *Billboard* chart for just one week.

April 1   Effectively the last day of recording on what had become a marathon set of sessions for *Sgt Pepper's Lonely Hearts Club Band*. On the same day Paul flew to Los Angeles and then onto Denver on Frank Sinatra's private Lear Jet to see Jane Asher. Near the end of his trip, while filming Jane on his home movie camera, Paul thought of the *Magical Mystery Tour* idea.

April 10   While in Los Angeles Paul visited Brian Wilson who was recording *Vegetables* for his legendary *Smile* project.

April 24   All the Beatles went to Donovan's opening night of his week at the Saville Theatre.

April 25   Work begins on the *Magical Mystery Tour* theme.

April 29   John visits the 14 Hour Technicolor Dream at Alexandra Palace, Yoko is performing but that was not the reason that John visited – he was also on an acid trip.

May 11   Sessions for *Baby You're A Rich Man*.

May 12   Radio London, the pirate ship in the North Sea plays the *Sgt Pepper's Lonely Hearts Club Band* album from start to finish.

May 15   Paul sees Georgie Fame at the Bag O' Nails club and meets Linda Eastman who was with Chas Chandler from the Animals; later they went to the Speakeasy where Paul heard Procol Harum's *A Whiter Shade of Pale* for the first time.

May 18   John and Paul sing backing vocals on the Rolling Stones, *We Love You* single.

May 19   The launch party for *Sgt Pepper's Lonely Hearts Club Band* is held at Brian Epstein's flat in London.

May 20   *Sgt Pepper's Lonely Hearts Club Band* is played in its entirety on the BBC, all except *A Day in The Life*, which the BBC banned.

May 24   The Beatles go to see Procol Harum at the Speakeasy.

June 1   UK album release. *Sgt Pepper's Lonely Hearts Club Band* on Parlophone PMC 7027 (mono) PCS 7027 (stereo).

June 2   US album release. *Sgt Pepper's Lonely Hearts Club Band* on Capitol MAS 2653 (mono) SMAS 2653 (stereo).

June 4   Paul is among the audience at the Saville Theatre where the Jimi Hendrix Experience perform the title track to *Sgt Pepper's Lonely Hearts Club Band* to open their set.

June 8	Rolling Stone Brian Jones is invited to a session at Abbey Road by Paul. Jones plays the sax solo on *You Know My Name (Look Up My Number.*
June 14	Work begins on *All You Need Is Love.*
June 24	A rehearsal and press call for the *Our World Live* show.
June 25	*Our World* live broadcast from Abbey Road.
July 3	John, Paul and George, with Cynthia, Pattie and Jane attend a private party for the Monkees.
July 7	UK single release *All You Need Is Love/Baby You're A Rich Man* on Parlophone R 5620.
July 17	US single release *All You Need Is Love/Baby You're A Rich Man* on Capitol 5964.
July 21	John's idea of the Beatles living together on an island has them all heading for Greece, along with wives and girlfriends (not Maureen as she was heavily pregnant) in search of the perfect place. By the end of the month they had all flown home having been unsuccessful.
July 22	*All You Need Is Love* spends the first of three weeks at No.1 in the UK.
August 1	George and Patti flew to Los Angeles renting a house on Blue Jay Way. George visits Ravi Shankar and takes more sitar lessons. They later visited San Francisco and George walked around Height-Ashbury.
August 19	Ringo and Maureen's second son, Jason is born. *All You Need Is Love* tops the *Billboard* chart for one week.
August 22	Work begins on *Your Mother Should Know.*
August 24	John, Cynthia, Paul, Jane, George and Pattie attend the Maharishi's lecture at the Hilton Hotel in London.
August 25	John, Paul, Jane, Ringo, George and Patti leave London's Euston Station with the Maharishi on a train bound for North Wales where they are to attend his lectures at a college in Bangor.
August 27	While the Beatles are in Bangor Brian Epstein is found dead in his flat in London. They all leave Wales to return to London.
August 29	Brian Epstein's family funeral at which none of the Beatles are in attendance.
September 5	After holding a meeting four days before at which they had decided to press on with *Magical Mystery Tour* the band starts work on *I Am The Walrus.*
September 11	After a week spent working on more tracks, including *Blue Jay Way*, the band and cast leave on the *Magical Mystery Tour* coach to begin filming in the West of England.

WORLD VOCAL GROUP

1	BEATLES	8234
2	Beach Boys	5648
3	Monkees	4297
4	Rolling Stones	1626
5	Bee Gees	1508
6	Jordanaires	1367
7	Four Tops	1100
8	Diana Ross/Supremes	965
9	Shadows	962
10	Seekers	539
11	Hollies	486
12	Jimi Hendrix Experience	373
13	Everly Brothers	351
14	Mamas and Papas	288
15	Kinks	278
16	Who	263
17	Troggs	262
18	Dave Clark Five	261
19	Small Faces	236
20	Traffic	227

September 15 The Beatles arrive back in London after filming in various locations.

September 18 Filming in London and in Kent over the following six days.

September 26 Recording *The Fool On The Hill* begins at Abbey Road.

October 11 Yoko Ono's one-woman show, *Yoko and Me*, the 'me' being John Lennon opens in London.

October 17 The Beatles attend Brian Epstein's memorial service at the New London Synagogue; Earlier in the day John and Cynthia went to the Motor Show at Earl's Court to buy a new car.

October 18 The première of *How I Won The War* in London attended by all four Beatles, their wives and girlfriends.

November 1 The last day of filming for *Magical Mystery Tour* that had been continuing intermittently for almost two months.

November 7 The last day of recording on *Magical Mystery Tour*.

November 17 The Beatles Ltd became Apple Music Ltd.

November 19 Jane and Paul went to see The Bee Gees, The Flowerpot Men, The Bonzo Dog Doo-Dah Band, and Tony Rivers & The Castaways at the Saville Theatre.

November 22 George starts work on his *Wonderwall* film soundtrack.

November 24 UK single release *Hello Goodbye/I Am The Walrus* on Parlophone R5655.

November 27 US single release *Hello Goodbye/I Am The Walrus* on Capitol 2056. US album release, *The Magical Mystery Tour* on Capitol MAL 2835 (mono) and SMAL 2835 (stereo).

December 3 Ringo flies to Rome to begin work on the movie *Candy*. Paul took Jane to his Scottish farmhouse on holiday.

December 8 UK EP release, *Magical Mystery Tour* on Parlophone MMT 1 (mono) and SMMT 1 (stereo).

December 9 *Hello Goodbye* spends the first of its seven weeks at No.1 in the UK.

December 17 Ringo's work on *Candy* ends.

December 21 *The Magical Mystery Tour* fancy dress party for cast and crew. Among the attendees are Mike Love and Bruce Johnston from the Beach Boys.

December 25 Paul and Jane announce their engagement.

December 26 *Magical Mystery Tour* premieres on BBC TV, naturally it's in black and white.

December 30 *Hello Goodbye* spends the first of three weeks at No.1 on the Billboard chart.

Fame at Last!

After spending three days working on *Penny Lane* John and Paul went to the Cromwellian Club in London to a fancy dress party hosted by Georgie Fame for his girlfriend Carmen Jiminez. John decided a Catholic priest from the 19th century was the look for him, while Paul was anxious that the 'South will rise again.' George like the other Beatles regularly went to see different artists perform; he is seen here emerging from the Royal Albert Hall where he and Paul had seen Donovan in concert.

ABOVE: *Donovan seen here at a Festival in the summer of 1967 was popular with Paul and George in particular.*

RIGHT: *Jimi Hendrix seen here in the summer of 1967 with British politician Jeremy Thorpe was seen by one or more of the Beatles several times during the year.*

Musical Mates

On 7 February Paul spent an evening at home in Cavendish Avenue with Monkee, Micky Dolenz – it was just one of many connections with a musical mate during the year. With less time spent on the road than in any previous year since the band had formed there was time to go and see others perform from the comfort of the stalls rather than the side of the stage.

ABOVE: *The Who at their most destructive in 1967 when John and Paul went to see them top the bill at the Saville Theatre in January.*

ABOVE: *John and Ringo went to see Chuck Berry and Del Shannon at the Saville Theatre in February.*

RIGHT AND BELOW: *Tony Rivers and the Castaways (right) who Paul went to see in late 1967 at the Saville Theatre where the Bee Gees (below) topped the bill.*

It's Wonderful To Be Here

On 12 May Radio London, the pirate ship anchored in the North Sea, stole a march on all of its competitors, the BBC included, by being the first radio station to play *Sgt Pepper's Lonely Hearts Club Band* in its entirety. A week later the band launched the album at a party at Brian Epstein's flat in Chapel Street in London's Mayfair. Among the press photographers was a 25 year old New Yorker named Linda Eastman.

"Don't forget that under this frilly shirt is a hundred year-old man who's seen and done so much – but at the same time knowing so little."

JOHN LENNON

"We have never thought about splitting up. We want to go on recording together. The Beatles live!"

RINGO

LEFT: *Paul chats with Jimmy Savile who like everyone else probably loved the cover of Sgt Pepper.*

ABOVE: *Linda Eastman asks the questions.*

BELOW: *Linda among the press photographers.*

"Whether the album is their best yet, I shouldn't like to say after one hearing. Whether it was worth the five months it took to make, I would argue. But it's a very good LP and will sell like hot cakes."

ALLEN EVANS — NEW MUSICAL EXPRESS

Their World

The BBC had the idea of hosting a satellite link up with 26 countries and who better to appear on it than the Beatles? The performance of the band and the orchestra were all mixed live on air on 25 June and the result is remarkable. All these pictures were taken the day before when 100 pressmen gathered in Abbey Road Studios after The Beatles and the 13-piece orchestra had done a run through on 24 June. Ringo's drum roll at the start of the *All You Need Is Love* is the only bit that was not live; he did it the following day. Parlophone rushed out the single on 7 July and Capitol had it out in America ten days later.

"This song will be our next single. This TV show will give it a nice send off."

JOHN LENNON

Did You Have
A Nice Trip?

It was John's idea that the Beatles should all live together on
an island, with four separate houses all surrounding a state
of the art recording studio. With this in mind all four Beatles
went to Greece in July, along with wives and girlfriends
(not Maureen as she was heavily pregnant) in search of
the perfect place to set up their musical Erewhon. By the
end of the month they had all flown home having been
unsuccessful. John had decided his Rolls Royce should be
painted in his own image.

Life and the Universe

John, Cynthia, George, Pattie, Paul and Jane all went to the Maharishi Mahesh Yogi's lecture at the Hilton Hotel in London's Park Lane on Thursday 24 August. Afterwards they had a private audience with the Maharishi and all three of the Beatles decided to head to Bangor in North Wales the following day where the Maharishi was holding a seminar over the weekend; they got Ringo to come along too. Sitting between Jane and John in the main photograph is Mike McCartney, Paul's brother. Just out of shot to Cynthia's right are George and Pattie's sister Jenny Boyd,

The Two Day
Trip to Bangor

There was such a large crowd at Euston Station the following day that Cynthia became separated from John and a policeman refused to let her through the barrier, which meant that Neil Aspinall had to drive her to North Wales.

Saturday was spent listening to the Maharishi's message. On the Sunday evening it was Jane Asher who took a call from London to say Brian Epstein was dead. Soon afterwards George, Ringo and John faced the press and Paul and Jane left to be driven home to London.

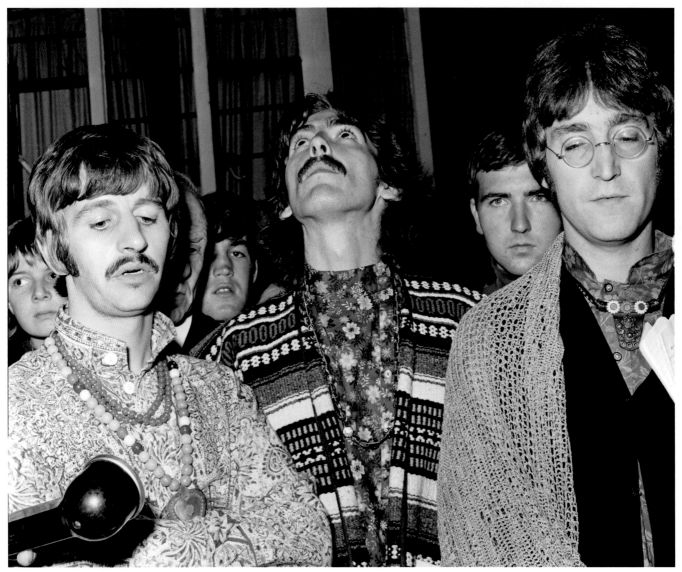

*"Our friend's
dead. How do
we handle this?"*

PAUL

*"Nothing you can do...
Bless him, wish him
well, get on with life."*

MAHARISHI MAHESH YOGI

The Man Who Made The Beatles?

All four Beatles, their wives and girlfriends, along with many other members of the bands, as well as solo artists, that Brian Epstein had managed attended the New London Synagogue for a memorial service on 17 October.

Roll up, Roll Up!

On 11 September the 43-seat *Magical Mystery Tour* coach left central London with Paul on board. It picked up George, John and Ringo in Virginia Water, close to where they lived, and then headed west, stopping in Winchester for lunch at the Pied Piper restaurant. In the evening it arrived in Teignmouth in Devon, where the band stayed at the Royal Hotel. The following day they tried to visit Widecombe Fair but the bus got stuck on a bridge and after lunch in Plymouth they checked into the Atlantic Hotel in Newquay where filming took place the following day. The coach returned to London on 15 September.

Editing the *Magical Mystery Tour* TV programme began on 24 September in Soho with Roy Benson (page 261) and the Beatles stopped into a local coffee bar and sang with a well known busker. It had been anticipated that the edit would take 2 weeks; it ended up taking 11. The programme aired on the BBC, in black and white of course, on 26 December. The critical response was underwhelming.

"Aren't we entitled to have a flop? It's hard because it's our first, but we'll get used to the idea. The lesson is good for us and we're not bitter about it. "

PAUL - 27 DECEMBER 1967

Openings

The day after Brian's memorial service all the Beatles, their wives and Jane Asher went to the premiere of John's film, *How I Won The War*. A month later the Beatles Ltd changed its name to Apple Music Ltd. Work was already underway on the boutique the band was to open on the corner of Baker Street and Paddington Street. The front and side of the building was decorated with a fabulous mural that had been designed and painted (with the help of several art students) by The Fool, a collective of three itinerant Dutch designers. In September 1967 the Beatles had given The Fool £100,000 to design and stock the new boutique. It opened on 5 December with just John and George the only Beatles attending; Ringo was in Rome filming *Candy* and Paul was in Scotland at his farm. The boutique was a financial disaster, closing eight months later.

Fancy That!

Four days before Christmas the Beatles held a fancy dress party at the Royal Lancaster Hotel for everyone involved in the making of *Magical Mystery Tour*, as well as some friends – the entertainment was provided by The Bonzo Dog Doo-Dah Band. Among the guests were Mike Love and Bruce Johnston from the Beach Boys who ended up singing on stage with the Beatles. . .it must have been some night.

1968

Alone Together

IT WAS A YEAR of being both alone and together. All the Beatles undertook major solo projects of one kind or another, with the exception of Ringo, although he had only just finished filming *Candy* – and even he made a solo guest appearance on Cilla Black's TV show. The fiasco that was Apple continued with none of the band really giving the requisite attention to their multi-faceted business empire. Yet from the mayhem rose *The White Album* as it has come to be called and despite the uncertainties *Hey Jude* topped the American singles chart for nine weeks, making it the longest reigning hit of the band's career.

1968 TIMELINE

January 5   *Magical Mystery Tour* was shown on BBC 2 in colour while George was working on his *Wonderwall* soundtrack; two days later he flew to India to work with local musicians.

January 17   The Beatles minus George, who was still away, went to a reception for Grapefruit, a band managed by Apple who had signed to RCA.

January 25   The band film their short appearance at the end of *Yellow Submarine*.

February 3   The band begin work on *Lady Madonna*, Paul's homage to Fat's Domino. The following day they work on John's, *Across the Universe*.

February 6   Ringo appears alone on Cilla Black's TV show for which Paul has supplied the theme song – *Step Inside Love*.

February 8   Comedian Spike Milligan, who George Martin had produced, watched the Beatles recording *Across The Universe* and they agreed he could use the song as the theme for a World Wildlife Charity album he was involved with.

February 15   John, Cynthia, George, Pattie and her sister Jenny flew Qantas to Delhi.

February 19   Paul, Jane, Ringo and Maureen followed on to India where the Beatles were going to stay at the Maharishi's ashram.

March 1   Ringo and Maureen leave Rishikesh.

March 15   UK single release *Lady Madonna/The Inner Light* on Parlophone R 5675.

March 18   US single release *Lady Madonna/The Inner Light* on Capitol 2138.

March 26   Paul and Jane returned to London from Rishikesh and headed for Paul's farm in Scotland.

March 30   *Lady Madonna* spends the first of two weeks at No.1 in the UK.

April 12   John, Cynthia, George and Pattie leave Rishikesh for reasons that have never fully been explained. John wrote *Sexy Sadie* about the Maharishi at Delhi airport on the way home.

May 5   Twiggy saw Mary Hopkin on *Opportunity Knocks*, a TV talent show, and suggested that Paul sign her to Apple the Beatles' new record label.

May 11   John and Paul flew to New York to meet with various people to launch Apple Corp Ltd. in America. Paul reconnected with New York photographer Linda Eastman.

May 15   George, Pattie, Ringo and Maureen went to Cannes for the premiere of *Wonderwall* as Paul and John were flying home from New York.

May 19   Yoko Ono visited John at Kenwood in Weybridge where they did some experimental recordings. When Cynthia returned home she apparently found Yoko wearing her robe.

May 30   Work began on The Beatles' new album. The band had met up at George's home to go over songs for their new album; much of the material was written in India and there was a lot of it! Work continued throughout June.

June 7   George and Ringo along with their wives flew to Los Angeles so that George could appear in a documentary about Ravi Shankar.

June 8   Paul was best man at his brother Mike's wedding.

June 15   John and Yoko appeared in public as a couple for the first time planting an acorn for peace in Coventry; three days later they attended the opening of the National Theatre production of *In His Own Write* directed by Victor Spinetti.

June 20   Paul attended a meeting of Capitol sales people in Los Angeles; he was joined by Linda Eastman who flew from New York to be with him.

June 30   Paul recorded the Black Dyke Mills Band in Saltaire near Bradford, performing one of Paul's compositions that would be released on Apple.

July 1   *The White Album* sessions continue and in the evening John and Yoko attend the opening of John's first solo art exhibition.

July 17   The premiere of *Yellow Submarine* is held at the London Pavillion in Piccadilly.

July 20   Jane Asher publically announces her engagement to Paul is off.

June 29   Work starts on *Hey Jude* at Abbey Road and continues over the next week at Trident Studios in Soho because they have an 8-track studio.

August 11 Apple Records is launched.

August 26 US single release *Hey Jude/Revolution* on Capitol as Apple 2276.

August 30 UK single release *Hey Jude/Revolution* on Parlophone as Apple R5722.

September 14 *Hey Jude* tops the UK singles chart for the first of its two weeks.

October 16 Having spent months working on the album the band spent a marathon 24 hours sequencing it ready for release. It was to be a double album.

October 28 Cynthia Lennon filed for divorce.

October 31 Linda Eastman moved to London with her daughter Heather.

November 22 UK album release *The Beatles* (aka *The White Album*) released on Parlophone as Apple PMC 7067/8 (mono) PCS 7067/8 (stereo).

November 25 US album release *The Beatles* released on Capitol as Apple SWBO 101 (stereo only).

November 28 John and Yoko found guilty of possession of cannabis.

November 29 John and Yoko's *Two Virgins* album is released.

December 10 John and Yoko attend rehearsals for the Rolling Stones *Rock and Roll Circus*, filming the programme the following day.

December 23 John and Yoko were Father and Mother Christmas at the Apple Christmas party at 3 Saville Row.

A Grapefruit for Apple

Grapefruit was a band that rose out of the ashes of Tony Rivers and the Castaways before signing to Apple on a management deal. Terry Doran, the 'man from the motor trade' managed them and they had a record deal with RCA who released *Dear Delilah* as their first single. To add to the hype it was announced that John and Paul helped produce it. On 17 January the Beatles less George, who was in India working on his *Wonderwall* soundtrack (he returned the following day), attended a party to launch the band, so too did Brian Jones, Donovan and Cilla Black. Ringo and Maureen (with poodle) had just flown back to London from Liverpool where they had been visiting family. Two weeks after the Grapefruit launch Ringo began rehearsing for his appearance on Cilla Black's new TV series.

A Little Meditation

On 15 February John and Cynthia Lennon, along with George and Pattie Harrison, and Pattie's sister Jenny, left London's Heathrow Airport to fly to India to visit the Maharishi Mahesh Yogi's ashram for a course in meditation. Paul and Jane with Ringo and Maureen followed three days later.

ABOVE: *The entrance to the ashram.*

Reward For Sgt Pepper

On 9 March with all the Beatles, except Ringo, still in Rishikesh it was announced that they had won four Grammy Awards for *Sgt Pepper's Lonely Hearts Club Band*. It triumphed in the Best Album, Best Contemporary Album, Best Album Cover and Best Engineered Album categories. Ringo was on hand at Abbey Road to give the award to the album's engineer, Geoff Emerick, watched by George Martin.

Apple in the Big Apple

John, Beatles associate Alexis Mardas (aka Magic Alex), Paul, and
John's driver Les Anthony at London Airport, 11 May 1968. John
and Paul were bound for New York to launch Apple in America.

Evolution or Revolution?

In late May the Beatles met at George Harrison's Esher home to go over what material they had between them for their next album – they had a lot, much of it written in India. Throughout June they worked on tracks for the new, as yet, untitled album, it was work that was to continue for months. In between the mammoth recording sessions all four members of the band undertook personal projects of their own. On an even more personal level John's marriage to Cynthia hit the rocks, Yoko was 'the other woman', meanwhile Paul's engagement to Jane was under pressure, in Paul's case Linda Eastman was getting his attention.

RIGHT: *Mike McCartney's wedding on 8 June – Jane Asher, Paul, Jim McCartney (father), Mike McCartney, and his new wife Angela, Angie McCartney (Jim's wife), bride's father and Ruth McCartney (Paul's stepsister).*

ABOVE: *Ringo, Maureen, George and Pattie went to Los Angeles on 8 June where George filmed a guest appearance in Ravi Shankar's film, Raga. Seen here returning 10 days later they are accompanied by Peter Asher (left, of Peter & Gordon fame, as well as being Jane's brother)*

ABOVE: *Paul with the Black Dyke Mills Band, in Saltaire, Yorkshire on 30 June. The band recorded a version of the McCartney instrumental Thingumybob that would be one of the first releases on Apple Records. Martha, Paul's Old English sheepdog is with him.*

LEFT AND ABOVE: *John and Yoko Ono pooled their artistic resources to create this piece of "sculpture" for an exhibition in the ruins of Coventry Cathedral. Unfortunately the organisers said it wasn't a sculpture and should not be placed among the work of well known sculptors that included Henry Moore and Barbara Hepworth. In the centre of the seat John and Yoko planted two acorns which were later stolen. The plaque which carried the name of the work "Yoko by John and John by Yoko" was also stolen soon afterwards. Three days later the couple made their relationship official when they attended the opening of the National Theatre production of In His Own Write directed by Victor Spinetti in London.*

THIS PAGE: *On 1 July while sessions for what would become the White Album continued John and Yoko attended the opening of John's first solo art exhibition. To mark the opening of You Are Here at Robert Fraser's Gallery, John let off 365 helium filled white balloons.*

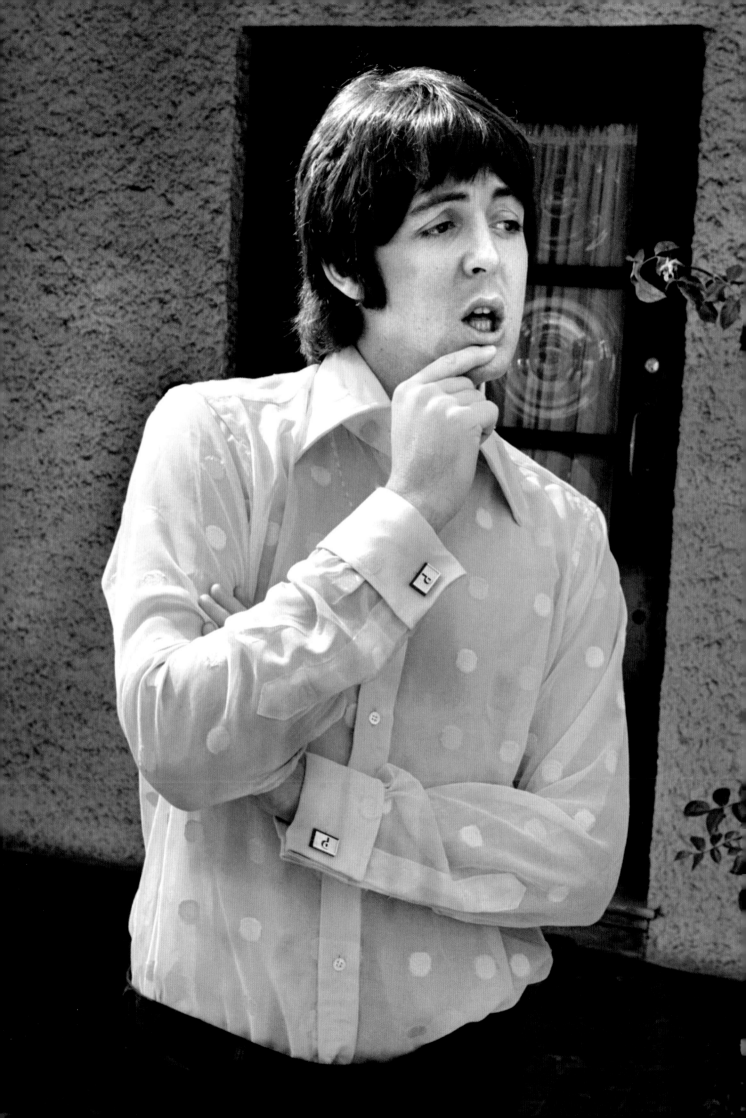

In The Land Where I Was Born?

On 17 July the premiere of *Yellow Submarine* was held at the London Pavilion in Piccadilly. All four Beatles attended with John bringing Yoko, and George and Maureen accompanied by their wives. Paul was alone. Three days later Jane Asher announced that their engagement was over.

RIGHT: *John and Yoko leave Marylebone Magistrates Court on 19 October after being remanded on bail on drugs charges.*

It's Only Rock and Roll

On 10 December there was a lunchtime press call at Intertel studios for the Rolling Stones *Rock and Roll Circus* TV production (anything The Beatles could do, The Stones could do too); besides The Rolling Stones, there was The Who, John Lennon along with Yoko and his son Julian, Eric Clapton and Marianne Faithfull.

After the press call, rehearsals and filming began with Yoko, dressed as a witch, with The Who, Jethro Tull, clowns, a tiger in a cage, Mick, dressed appropriately as a ringmaster along with the rest of the Stones in various outfits. When the music began John Lennon, Eric Clapton, Mitch Mitchell (drummer with Jimi Hendrix's Experience) and Keith Richards played *Yer Blues*. Keith played the bass in this 'supergroup' that was christened the Dirty Mac band. Later John, Mick and Eric played *Peggy Sue*, while Lennon did a wry version of Elvis', *It's Now Or Never*.

"If anyone had told me we would have been doing this kind of thing six years ago I would have said they were mad."

BRIAN JONES

1969

The End?

EVERYTHING HAS A beginning and so it also must end. The Beatles break up was much like every other break up, it had a start, a middle and an end. There are some that argue it was Brian's passing, others that it was Yoko's arrival, while others make the case that it had just run its course. Whatever the truth, the sand was gradually running out of the jar all the way through this year. However, no matter what the Beatles were arguing about they always had the ability to make great music. While some of it was music by rote other songs they recorded in this strangest of years were among the best of their career.

1969 TIMELINE

January 2 At Twickenham Studios the Beatles begin filming *Get Back*, for a number of days in January. It was not a happy time.

January 3 American Customs officials impound 10,000 copies of John and Yoko's *Two Virgins* saying it is "pornographic."

January 13 UK album release, *Yellow Submarine* on Capitol as Apple SW 385.

January 17 US album release, *Yellow Submarine* on Parlophone as Apple PMC 7070 (mono) PCS 7070 (stereo).

January 18 John tells a journalist that the Beatles could be broke in six months.

January 20 The idea of a live concert is shelved and the filming of *Get Back* is moved to the Beatles incomplete Apple Studios in the basement of 3 Saville Row.

January 22 Work continues on filming and recording the *Get Back* sessions at Apple. George Martin had brought in two 4 track machines and Billy Preston, a veteran of Little Richard's band who the Beatles knew from Hamburg joins the sessions on keyboards.

January 28 *Get Back* and *Don't Let Me Down* are recorded, both sides of the band's next single. Later in the day John and Yoko met with Allen Klein, who had been managing the Rolling Stones affairs, and agreed that Klein should be his personal advisor.

January 30 The Beatles play live on the roof of the Apple building – their last live appearance as a band.

February 2 Yoko's divorce from Anthony Cox is finalised.

February 3 Ringo begins his 13 weeks of filming *The Magic Christian* at Twickenham Studios with Peter Sellers. Allen Klein appointed as the Beatles business manager. Linda Eastman's father, John is appointed as Apple's General Counsel to keep a close eye on Allen Klein at Paul's request.

February 17 James Taylor's Apple album, produced by Peter Asher is released.

February 21 Mary Hopkin's *Postcard* album is released; Paul produces it.

February 24 It's announced that a merchant bank has got control of Epstein's NEMS Enterprises. The Beatles are not happy.

March 12 Paul and Linda get married; four days later they fly to America for three weeks.

March 20 John and Yoko try to marry on a cross channel ferry but are refused permission. They fly to Paris and then to Gibraltar, where they marry, before flying back to Paris.

March 21 The Jackie Lomax album, *Is This What You Want*, produced by George, is released on Apple.

March 25 The day after having lunch with Salvador Dali in Paris John and Yoko fly to Amsterdam to begin their seven day Bed-in for Peace at the Hilton Hotel.

March 31 After their Amsterdam Bed-in John and Yoko fly to Vienna where they hold a press conference in a bag. The Apple press office sends out acorns for Peace to every world leader.

April 2 John and Paul meet with the merchant bankers to try to retain control of Northern Songs, as Dick James wants to sell his shares to ATV.

April 3 John and Yoko are interviewed in a white bag on the Eamonn Andrews TV show.

April 11 UK single release *Get Back/Don't Let Me Down* on Parlophone as Apple R 5777.

April 14 John and Paul recorded *The Ballad of John And Yoko* at Abbey Road without the other two Beatles – Ringo was still filming and George was abroad.

April 16 Recording *Old Brown Shoe* at Abbey Road, finished on April 18, along with tracks that will appear on Abbey Road during the rest of the month.

April 22 John changes his middle name from Winston to Ono by deed poll.

April 24 The BBC's *Top Of The Pops* shows a clip of *Get Back* filmed on the roof of Apple.

April 26 *Get Back* tops the UK singles chart for the first of its 6 six weeks at No.1

May 2 The band work on George's song, *Something*.

May 4 John and Yoko buy a new home, Tittenhurst Park in Sunninghill, Berkshire. Ringo hosts a wrap party with Peter Sellers at a club in London, John, Yoko, Paul and Linda attend.

May 5 US single release, *Get Back/Don't Let Me Down* on Capitol as Apple 2490.

May 8 Allen Klein sacks Alistair Taylor, Brian's former assistant who was the GM of Apple. John, George and Ringo sign a management contract with Klein, Paul does not.

May 9 The Beatles have a flaming row over Klein at Olympic Studios in Barnes. Paul continues to hold out and John, Ringo and George walk out and leave Paul to record *My Dark Hour* with the Steve Miller Band.

May 9   UK album release *Unfinished Music No.2: Life With The Lions* by John and Yoko is released as Zapple 01; George's Electronic Sound (released the same day) is Zapple 02.

May 16   Ringo and Maureen travel on the newly completed *QE II* to New York with Peter Sellers; John was refused a US visa because of his drug conviction, so he and Yoko cannot travel.

May 24   John and Yoko fly to the Bahamas where Ringo and Maureen are on holiday. They plan a Bed-in as it's the closest they can get to America without entering the country.

May 24   *Get Back* spends the first of five weeks at No.1 in America

May25   Deciding that the Bahamas are too hot John and Yoko fly to Toronto.

May26   US album release *Unfinished Music No.2: Life With The Lions* by John and Yoko is released as Zapple ST 3357.

May 30   UK single release *The Ballad of John and Yoko/Old Brown Shoe* on Parlophone as Apple R5786.

June 1   In their hotel suite John and Yoko record *Give Peace a Chance* along with a chorus of guests including Tommy Smothers, Timothy Leary and Petula Clark. After the Bed-in finishes John and Yoko return to London.

June 4   US single release *The Ballad Of John And Yoko/Old Brown Shoe* on Capitol as Apple 2531.

June 14   *The Ballad Of John And Yoko* tops the UK singles charts for the first of 3 weeks at No.1

June 29   John, Yoko, her daughter Kyoko and John's son Julian head off for a motoring holiday in Scotland. On 1 July they have an accident that sees them all detained in hospital.

July 3   Paul working at Abbey Road on *Abbey Road*. Ringo and Maureen deputise for John and Yoko at a launch party for *Give Peace A Chance*.

July 4   UK single release *Give Peace A Chance/Remember Love* by The Plastic Ono Band on Apple 13.

July 7   US single release *Give Peace A Chance/Remember Love* by The Plastic Ono Band on Apple 1809.

July 9   With Yoko laying on a bed in Abbey Road the band work on *Maxwell's Silver Hammer*. Work continued on *Abbey Road* for much of the month.

August 22   US single release, *Hare Krishna Mantra* by the Radha Krishna Temple, produced by George on Apple 1810.

August 25   *Abbey Road* is finally complete.

August 28   Paul and Linda's daughter Mary is born. George and the Radha Krishna Temple launch their record at a house in Sydenham, Kent.

August 31   George, Pattie, Ringo, Maureen, John and Yoko all travel to the Isle of Wight to see Bob Dylan perform the next day.

September 13   The Plastic Ono Band play live at the Toronto Rock 'n' Roll Festival with just one day's notice. With John and Yoko are Eric Clapton, Klaus Voormann and drummer Alan White.

September 20   John tells the others at a business meeting with Allen Klein that he's leaving the band.

September 26   UK album release of *Abbey Road* on Parlophone as Apple PCS 7088 (stereo only).

October 1   US album release of *Abbey Road* on Capitol as Apple SO 383 (stereo only).

October 6   US single release, *Something/Come Together* on Capitol as Apple 2564.

October 12   After four days in hospital Yoko miscarries.

October 20   US single release *Cold Turkey/Don't Worry Kyoko (Mummy's Only Looking For A Hand In The Snow)* by the Plastic Ono Band on Apple 1813.

October 24   UK single release *Cold Turkey? /Don't Worry Kyoko (Mummy's Only Looking For A Hand In The Snow)* by the Plastic Ono Band on Apple 1003.

October 27   Ringo starts work on his solo album, *Sentimental Journey*.

October 31   UK single release, *Something/Come Together* on Parlophone as Apple R5814.

November 25   John returns his MBE to Her Majesty the Queen.

Dcember 2   George joins the Delaney and Bonnie and Friends tour.

December 9   John and Yoko announce they are to make a film about convicted killer James Hanratty.

December 10   Ringo, Maureen, John and Yoko attend the premiere of *The Magic Christian*.

December 12   UK album release, *The Plastic Ono Band– Live Peace In Toronto* on Apple CORE 2001.

December 15   The Plastic Ono band play the Lyceum Ballroom in London.

December 31   George, Patti, Paul and Linda attend Ringo and Maureen's New Year's Eve party; John and Yoko are spreading their peace message in Denmark.

Two weddings...

Paul announced his engagement to Linda Eastman to the press in February, ironically accompanied by Peter Asher. Paul and Linda, accompanied by Linda's daughter Heather got married on 12 March at Marylebone Register Office and afterwards they went to St John's Wood parish church where the Rev. Noel Perry-Gore blessed their union. Four days later John and Yoko flew to Paris with the intention of marrying. Unfortunately the French authorities refused them permission, for the simple reason that they had not lived in France long enough! They attempted to get married on a cross channel ferry on 20 March but that too failed so they flew to Gibraltar where they were married and within the hour they had flown back to Paris for their honeymoon at the Plaza Athenée.

...And A Bed-In

In room 902 of the Amsterdam Hilton John and Yoko began their Bed-in for peace on 25 March. They stayed there for seven days and left on 31 March to fly to Vienna where they held a press conference from inside a white bag. Bag-ism was the new Bed-ism.

The Magic Christian

At the beginning of February Ringo began what amounted to almost three months of work on a film that co-starred Peter Sellers. On 4 May Ringo hosted a wrap party with Peter Sellers at a club in London; John, Yoko, Paul and Linda all attend.

From Little Acorns

On 1 April John and Yoko flew back to London and hosted a press conference at Heathrow and talked about sending out acorns for peace to every world leader.

"Please plant these for peace. It will be the most positive thing they have done for peace for 200 years."

JOHN LENNON

On Holiday with the Lions

On 29 June, John, Yoko, her daughter Kyoko and John's son Julian left for a motoring holiday in Scotland. On 1 July while John was driving they had an accident. Their car ran into a ditch when a German motorist came around the corner on the wrong side of the road. All four of them were detained in hospital.

Hare Krishna!

Homage To His Bobness

In the month after Woodstock Bob Dylan appeared at the Isle of Wight Festival; The Band, who had appeared at the upstate New York Festival, to great acclaim, backed him. John, George and Ringo along with their wives went to the island to watch Dylan perform.

Goodbyes

A few days after Dylan's festival appearance
George and Patti saw Dylan and his wife off on
their flight back to America.

On 25 November John returned his MBE to Her Majesty the Queen.

*"Your Majesty, I am returning my
MBE as a protest against Britain's
involvement in the Nigeria–Biafra
thing, against our support of
America in Vietnam and against
'Cold Turkey' slipping down the
charts. With love, John Lennon."*

December - A Time for Peace

LEFT: *On 2 December George joined the Delaney and Bonnie and Friends tour at Bristol's Colston Hall. George with Delaney (next to George) Eric Clapton is seated on the chair. Saxophonist Bobby Keys is 2nd from left, Carl Radle far left and Bobby Whitlock, far right. Bonnie you can guess!*

RIGHT: *The Plastic Ono band at the Lyceum Ballroom in London on 15 December. It was mostly Delaney and Bonnie and friends with the addition of George, drummers Alan White and Keith Moon, Klaus Voormann and Billy Preston.*

ABOVE: *The day before their Lyceum concert this may possibly be John and Yoko in a bag at Speaker's Corner in London protesting against James Hanratty's conviction for murder.*

RIGHT: *John and Yoko switching from white to black to fly to Toronto, the day after their concert at the Lyceum, for a stay at Ronnie Hawkins' ranch where they telephoned radio stations around the world with a message of peace.*

Scotch SP 10-2500
Scotch SP 10-2500
Scotch SP 10-2500
Scotch SP 10-2500

10-2500

10-2500

1970

And It Was

FROM LIVING in each other's pockets, cadging each other's cigarettes, sharing a million laughs and being great mates, the Beatles became, if not the worst of enemies, then far from the best of friends — at least John, George and Ringo were on one side and Paul was on the other. The Beatles saw little of each other in 1970, it was like a messy divorce. Perhaps worst of all they even lost faith in the music they had tried to create together as a band. In many respects *Let it Be* was a disaster... and it was. The greatest group in the history of popular music were no more.

1970 TIMELINE

January 3 Paul, George and Ringo working on the *Let It Be* soundtrack at Abbey Road.

January 15 John's *Bag One* lithograph exhibition opens in London, the following day police raid the gallery and confiscate some of his erotic art. They are later returned after the gallery argues that Picasso's erotic art was not confiscated.

January 20 John and Yoko have their hair cropped in Copenhagen, fly hone five days later after almost a month in Denmark.

January 30 *Rolling Stone* publishes an interview with John and concludes the Beatles are splitting.

February 4 John and Yoko go to meet Malcolm X, the Black Power leader.

February 6 UK single release, *Instant Karma (We All Shine On)/Who Has Seen The Wind* by The Plastic Ono Band (A side) and Yoko Ono Lennon (B side) on Apple1003.

February 11 John and The Plastic Ono Band tape an appearance on *Top Of The Pops*.

February 19 US single release, *Instant Karma (We All Shine On)/Who Has Seen The Wind* by The Plastic Ono Band (A side) and Yoko Ono Lennon (B side) on Apple1818.

February 21 Paul works at Abbey Road on the eight track tapes for his solo album.

February 26 US album release of *Hey Jude* on Capitol as Apple SW385.

March 6 UK single release *Let It Be/You Know My Name (Look up my number)* on Parlophone as Apple R5833. *Govinda* by Radha Krishna Temple, produced by George on Apple 25.

March 6 US single release *Let It Be/You Know My Name (Look up my number)* on Capitol as Apple 2764.

March 12 George and Pattie move to Friar Park in Henley-on-Thames.

March 15 Ringo shoots a promo film for his *Sentimental Journey* album at London's Talk of the Town nightclub.

March 19 BBC TV's *Top Of The Pops* show a clip of the *Let It Be* film.

March 23 Paul finished mixing the master tapes of his solo album, *McCartney*.

March 24 US release of *Govinda* by Radha Krishna Temple on Apple 1821.

March 25 Phil Spector works on remixing some of the *Let It Be* tracks, which continues into April.

March 27 UK album release of Ringo's *Sentimental Journey* on Apple PCS 7101.

April 1 Phil Spector records a 50-piece orchestra at Abbey Road for some of the *Let It Be* tracks, including *The Long And Winding Road*.

April 10 Paul releases a press release about his solo album in which he announces he has left the Beatles. The news makes front pages around the world.

May 8 UK album release *Let It Be* on Parlophone as Apple PCS 7096 (stereo only).

May 11 US single release *The Long And Winding Road/For You Blue* on Capitol as Apple 2832.

May13 The *Let It Be* movie premieres in New York.

May 8 US album release *Let It Be* on Capitol as Apple AR 34001 (stereo only).

May 20 *Let it Be* premieres in Liverpool and London – there are no Beatles in attendance.

June 13 *The Long And Winding Road* spends the first of two weeks at No.1 in America.

Power To The people

John and Yoko, with their new short hair cuts arrived at the Holloway home of Malcolm X, the Black Power leader to swap their shorn hair for a pair of Muhammad Ali's boxing shorts covered in blood stains. Their idea was to auction the shorts for world peace. John and Yoko's hair was to be sold off and the proceeds given to the Black community in London.

Solo Works

While Paul and Linda, along with the sheep dog Martha, went to his farm in Campbeltown, prior to Paul mixing his solo album at Abbey Road, George and Pattie had moved house to the massive gothic mansion in Henley on Thames named Friar Park. Musically George was occupied with a second Radha Krishna Temple single on Apple prior to him getting down to the serious work of creating his masterpiece, *All Things Must Pass*.

1252

DAILY Mirror

5d. · Friday, April 10, 1970 · · · · No. 20,616

Kidnappers send girl home by taxi

PAUL QUITS THE BEATLES

McCartney . . . a deadlock over policy with John Lennon

CAROLE BENAINOUS, the little girl pictured with her mother yesterday, was held by kidnappers for more than twenty hours.

But the kidnappers sent six-year-old Carole home by taxi after her wealthy father had left £2,000 ransom money on a lonely road outside Paris.

The drama began on Wednesday when Carole and her mother, Madame Jeanine Benainous, stopped a taxi outside their Paris home to take Carole to school.

The driver was a kidnapper—

and he drove Carole to a secret hideout outside the city.

Four hours later the kidnappers rang Carole's home demanding the money for her release. They rang again twice through the night.

After the third call, Carole's company director father Rene decided to follow the kidnappers' instructions. He told police to keep away, drove to the pre-arranged spot, and left the cash.

A few hours later Carole returned home. She was unharmed, but very tired.

Last night a massive police hunt was going on for the kidnappers.

By DON SHORT

PAUL McCARTNEY has quit the Beatles. The shock news must mean the end of Britain's most famous pop group, which has been idolised by millions the world over for nearly ten years.

Today 28-year-old McCartney will announce his decision, and the reasons for it, in a no-holds-barred statement.

It follows months of strife over policy in Apple, the Beatles' controlling organisation, and an ever-growing rift between McCartney and his song-writing partner, John Lennon.

McCartney and Lennon are rated one of the greatest popular songwriting teams of the century.

But there is little doubt that McCartney's decision will bring it to an end.

Safe

In his statement, which consists of a series of answers to questions, McCartney says:

"I have no future plans to record or appear with The Beatles again. Or to write any more music with John."

Last night the statement was locked up in a safe at Apple headquarters in Savile-row, Mayfair—in the very rooms where the Beatles' break-up began.

The Beatles decided to appoint a "business adviser." Eventually they settled for American Allen Klein.

His appointment was strongly resisted by Paul, who sought the job for his father-in-law, American attorney Lee Eastman.

After a meeting in London Paul was out-voted 3-1 by John, and the other Beatles, George Harrison and Ringo Starr.

In his statement today Paul will say what he feels

'Deeply cut up' after policy row

about it all and his attitudes towards Mr. Klein.

Since the Klein appointment, Paul has refused to go to the Apple offices to work daily.

He kept silent and stayed at his St. John's Wood home with his photographer wife Linda, her daughter Heather, and their own baby Mary. He was obviously deeply cut up.

Close friends tried to pacify John and Paul. But August last year was the last time they were to work together — when they collaborated on the "Abbey Road" album.

One friend said: "The atmosphere is distinctly cool. They do not hate one another. This is just deadlock over policy."

Geniuses

Dick James, managing director of Northern Songs, publishers of the Lennon-McCartney songs, told me:

"It could mean that in competition with each other they will even write greater songs. They are both geniuses—Paul a melodic one and John in an inventive capacity."

There were other elements

that hastened Paul's decision to quit. John Lennon, on his marriage to Yoko Ono, set out on projects of his own. Ringo went into films, and George stepped in as a record producer.

Today McCartney will reveal his own plans for a solo programme.

It will include a full-length film based on the much-loved children's book character Rupert.

Secret

But the very first project is an album of his own compositions.

It is simply called "McCartney" which he not only wrote, but produced entirely himself.

He played every instrument to be heard on the 14 tracks. His wife Linda added vocal harmonies.

"The whole operation has been in secret. When the first 200 copies were pressed this week McCartney collected them all from the factory—so they could not be "poached."

By tomorrow hundreds of thousands will be rushed across the world. The first should reach Britain's shops by Monday morning.

DISC
and MUSIC ECHO 1s

APRIL 18, 1970   EVERY THURSDAY   USA 25c

Grateful Dead fly in – for one live date!

EXCLUSIVE DISC PICTURE BY LINDA McCARTNEY

Let him be!

PAUL McCARTNEY, who fled London last Friday leaving behind him a furore of doubt and rumour about his future following his "Quit The Beatles" bombshell, was back from a secret hideaway in the country on Sunday—ready to work the first project for his new company.

Paul, wife Linda, and children Heather and Mary, left their Cavendish Avenue, St. John's Wood, house in the early hours of Friday—the day the world learned, via Paul's specially - prepared handout, of the Beatle's decision to split from John, George and Ringo.

A close friend of Paul's told Disc: "He's not giving ANY interviews at the moment. In fact, fans and other people have been making his life a bit of a misery lately by 'picketing' his pad. I wish they'd let him alone to live his own life now."

Paul has — through his American lawyers, led by father-in-law Lee Eastman —bought exclusive rights to "Rupert Bear," the traditional children's story, for his newly-formed McCartney Productions. Paul plans to produce and write the music for a full-length animated cartoon film titled "Rupert."

But an Apple office spokesman told Disc: "At the moment Paul and 'Rupert' are still only in the planning stages. We have no further details."

"McCartney," Paul's first solo LP, is officially released tomorrow (Friday) and has a 19,000 advance order.

Full story behind the split and LP review, turn to pages 10 and 11.

GRATEFUL DEAD, one of America's top underground groups, are now definitely set for their first-ever British date next month. Country Joe and the Fish are also fixed for a visit at the same time.

Dead, whose current line-up is Jerry Garcia (lead guitar), Bob Weir (rhythm), Phil Lesh (bass) Bill Kreutzmann (drums), Ron McKernan (congas/organ), and Mickey Hart (percussion), are exclusively-signed for the giant open-air "Hollywood Music Festival" near Newcastle - under - Lyme, Staffordshire, over the Whitsun, May 22-24, weekend.

Says Elliot Cohen, of the Red Bus Company, promoters of the festival: "It's a great scoop for us. We've been negotiating for the group since January."

Grateful Dead fly into London from Los Angeles on Friday, May 22, and make their only UK appearance at the festival on Sunday (24). They return to the States the next day. Country Joe appear on the Saturday Show.

Also on the "Hollywood" bill—as already reported—are Family, Traffic, Ginger Baker's Air Force, Colosseum, Free, Radha Krishna Temple, Trader Horne, Quintessence, James Gang, Black Sabbath, Black Widow.

Why Dana is bound to be a star . . . .
page 9

Flock arrive page 15

But Did The Singles...

As we all now know the world did not stop turning, there was to be more music and some great music at that. Since The Beatles stopped being The Beatles just about every great band has in some way been compared to the Fab Four. Their legacy lives on, their music will be forever and as long as aspiring young bands try to get a toehold on the ladder of success they will all secretly hoping to be...the next Beatles.

...Add Up To The Sum of The Parts?

Acknowledgements

The without whom department would like to thank Andy Neill who is one of the world's greatest Beatles experts. Andy kept me right when I veered off course, but any errors that remain are most definitely my own. Dave and Angela Ball turned my manuscript into a work of art. Thanks too are due to my great pal Richard Evans who is not only a talented designer but he also saw The Beatles above Burton's the tailors in the High Street Rhyll on 14 July 1962 (lucky devil!). Also thank you Simon Forty and Alan Greene at Compendium who love their music, and are jolly fine publishers. Thank you to Stackridge for their fine song, *Something About The Beatles*. You'll find it on their CD, *Something For The Weekend* – you will not be disappointed.

Thanks also to everyone at Mirrorpix, in particular Fergus McKenna, David Scripps, Mel Knight, Manjit Sandhu, John Mead, Vito Inglese and Alex Walters.

A big thank you to Bruce Johnston who is not only a Grammy Award winning songwriter but also a great guy who is a generous and good friend.

Finally thanks to The Beatles of course – without whom the world would have been a very different and much duller place to grow up in all those years ago. Was it really twenty years ago today?